PIRATES
OF
VIRGINIA

PIRATES
OF
VIRGINIA

PLUNDER AND
HIGH ADVENTURE
ON THE
OLD DOMINION COASTLINE

Mark P. Donnelly and Daniel Diehl

STACKPOLE
BOOKS

Published by
STACKPOLE BOOKS
5067 Ritter Road
Mechanicsburg, PA 17055
www.stackpolebooks.com

Printed in the United States of America

10 9 8 7 6 5 4 3 2 1

FIRST EDITION

Cover design by Wendy A. Reynolds
Cover photo by Mark P. Donnelly

Library of Congress Cataloging-in-Publication Data

Donnelly, Mark, 1967–
  Pirates of Virginia : plunder and high adventure on the Old Dominion
coastline / Mark P. Donnelly and Daniel Diehl. — First edition.
    pages cm
  Includes bibliographical references.
  ISBN 978-0-8117-1036-7 (pbk.)
  1. Pirates—Virginia—Atlantic Coast—History. 2. Pirates—Virginia—Atlantic Coast—Biography. 3. Pirates—Chesapeake Bay (Md. and Va.)—History. 4. Pirates—Chesapeake Bay (Md. and Va.)—Biography. 5. Virginia—History—Colonial period, ca. 1600-1775. 6. Atlantic Coast (Va.)—History, Naval. 7. Chesapeake Bay (Md. and Va.)—History, Naval. I. Diehl, Daniel. II. Title.
  F229.D74 2012
  910.4'5—dc23
                              2011051577

Contents

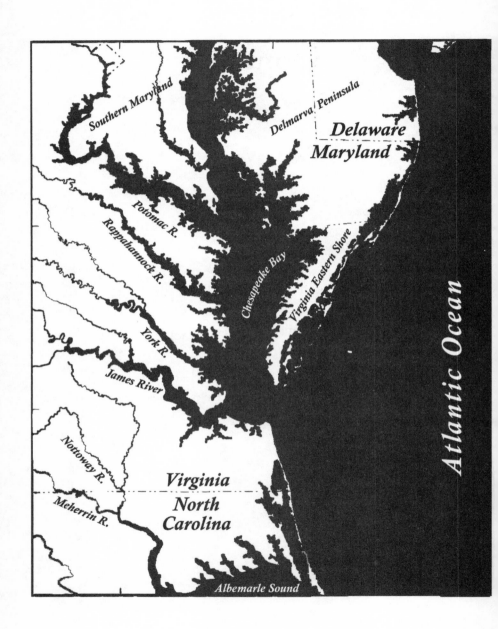

Introduction

The history of piracy in North America is rich and diverse. All the way from Nova Scotia, Canada, down to the Florida Keys and across the Gulf coast into Mexico, pirates, privateers, and buccaneers have hoisted the black flag in pursuit of booty and plunder. The Pacific coast and Great Lakes once saw their share of piracy as well, but it was along the Atlantic coast that many of the most infamous names from the Golden Age of Piracy conducted their disreputable trade.

Of all the harbors on the Atlantic coast, few places saw more conflict—or collusion—with pirates than the coastline of Virginia. We cannot hope to cover the long history of piracy in Virginia waters thoroughly in this slim volume, so we have selected representative stories that illustrate this diverse and often overlooked aspect of American history. But before we turn to the subject of piracy in Virginia, it is worth taking a moment to look at the history of piracy in general.

No single nation, race, or nationality ever held a monopoly on piracy. Piracy has existed wherever the rewards of the crime have been worth the risk of punishment. It is not difficult to imagine that the earliest humans to put to sea in boats were soon followed by the first pirates, intent on taking from the isolated and hence vulnerable exploratory sailors anything they might deem valuable. The Cretans, Phoenicians, and Vikings all tried their hand at piracy, and for centuries, the Barbary Corsairs of North Africa plundered shipping vessels across the Mediterranean and out into the open Atlantic. But it was the Europeans of the Atlantic seaboard—the French, Dutch, Spanish, Portuguese, and especially the British—who developed piracy into its most refined form. The burgeoning of British maritime trade in Tudor times (roughly 1500 to 1600 AD) led to a corresponding increase in

1

piracy in British waters. By the middle of the seventeenth century, there was hardly a fisherman off the coasts of Britain who did not at least dabble in the "sweet trade," and the pirates openly displayed their plundered wares for sale on deck.

The tiny country of Wales was virtually a pirate principality, and the inhabitants of the Cinque Ports on England's southeast coast sailed forth to plunder any ship passing within their greedy reach. Noblemen like Sir Richard Grenville, the earl of Pembroke (1542–91), and Sir John Killigrew, president of the Commissioners for Piracy (1507–67), maintained control of pirate syndicates all around the British coast.

From time to time, pirates found it profitable to offer their services to nations at war, and in this role they functioned more or less as legal naval auxiliaries under the general name of "privateers." These privateers operated under officially issued "letters of marque," which allowed them to attack any and all enemy shipping. The practice of privateering dates back to the thirteenth century, and it grew in frequency and popularity until it reached its zenith in the late seventeenth century. At this time, Britain and France were almost constantly at war with Spain in the New World. Privateers were commissioned to help break Spain's stranglehold on vast swaths of territory and lucrative maritime trade in the Americas. Inspired by Sir Francis Drake's raids on the Spanish Armada, English adventurers, as well as the French and Dutch, constantly harassed the Caribbean and Pacific seaboards of Spanish America. Their greatest success was Sir Henry Morgan's 1671 raid on Panama City, the richest town of the Spanish-American empire.

The distinction between these sea wolves and the pirates who followed them was, often as not, nothing more than a matter of legal terminology. The Spanish rejected all linguistic niceties and flatly called them all *piratas*. Understandably, the pirates who were dedicated primarily to plundering Spanish ships regarded themselves as a special brand of privateers. They termed themselves "buccaneers"—or, more precisely, *boucaniers*, meaning "smoker of meat" in French. And that is really what most of them were—simple herdsmen and woodsmen from the Caribbean island of Hispaniola, where they smoked and cured meat for preservation. Once these men turned their hands to sea roving, they insisted that their activities were perfectly legal, since all of their depredations, no matter how piratical in character or nature, were directed only against the Spanish. The British and French acquiesced in accepting this overly loose interpretation. The British even appointed the pirate Sir Henry Morgan to serve as lieutenant governor of Jamaica.

Yet the distinction between privateers, buccaneers, and pirates always remained blurred. Certainly, there was little veracity to the buccaneers' claim that they attacked only ships flying the Spanish flag. And how does one classify Englishmen and Frenchmen who, as the buccaneers did, plundered Spanish ships with equal zeal in peacetime as well as wartime? Did that make them pirates one day and privateers the next?

In 1704, the Reverend Cotton Mather, an American Puritan minister, warned his Boston congregation that "the privateering stroke so easily degenerates into the piratical, and the privateering trade is usually carried on with an unchristian temper and proves an inlet into so much debauchery and iniquity." A century later, in 1804, when piracy as such had largely vanished but plenty of privateers remained, Britain's greatest naval hero, Admiral Horatio Nelson, complained that "the conduct of all privateers is, as far as I have seen, so near piracy that I only wonder any civilized nation can allow them."

That peculiarly Caribbean form of privateer-come-pirate known as the buccaneer virtually died out after England made peace with Spain in 1689. By then, many veterans of buccaneering had turned to outright piracy, and their ranks were soon swollen by all kinds of disaffected sailors anxious to improve their miserable lot through the acquisition of illegally obtained riches. From the Caribbean, these sea rovers spread through virtually every sea and ocean around the world like a virus. And they prospered well.

Why were they so successful? The seventeenth century was a period of massive global expansion in oceangoing mercantile trade. By the end of that century, ports and trading posts had been established along most of the inhabited coastlines of the world, and a multitude of ships of all shapes, sizes, and nationalities navigated the vulnerable shipping lanes bearing both moderately and extremely valuable cargoes. With the significant lack of naval policing or law enforcement, these wealthy, lightly protected cargo ships made tempting targets and relatively easy prey.

But pirate plunder was valuable only if it could find a ready market where it could be sold or exchanged for needed goods and services. And it was North America that provided the most significant market. During the Golden Age of Piracy (roughly 1680–1730), pirates operated with the active support and cooperation of colonial governors, local officials, merchants, and the general populace of most of the North American colonies. In England, pirates were hunted down relentlessly. In American ports, however, they received protection, hospitality, ships, provisions, crews, counterfeit letters of marque, and most important, a place to sell their ill-gotten booty. For their part, the colonists also made a profit from the pirates' haul. Furthermore, by tacitly condoning piracy, the Americans struck a significant blow against British rule in a growing struggle that eventually culminated in the Revolutionary War. By dealing with pirates, the American colonies could acquire and trade in foreign commodities and luxury goods without paying British taxes on their import or delivery.

Among the particular circumstances that turned the Americans into a nation of "pirate brokers" was a series of Navigation Acts passed by the English government beginning in 1651. Originally, these acts were designed to protect British shipping interests from Dutch competition. The acts stipulated that virtually no goods could be imported into England or her colonies except in British ships manned by British crews. Moreover, most colonial imports and exports had to come from, and go to, England alone. The effect was to create a near monopoly for the mother kingdom in both shipping and trade, not to mention the taxes and excises on the goods.

Consequently, many American colonials felt exploited by this enforced trade with England at prices fixed by English merchants, who routinely purchased cheaply and sold dearly. At the same time, England did not supply everything the American colonists wanted and needed. On the other hand, the American shipping trade with the mother country could not prosper, because the English market was too small to absorb all of America's surplus goods, such as cotton, tobacco, indigo, and other agricultural products. As a result, the colonists responded by encouraging smuggling and piracy. The tobacco planters of Virginia and Maryland disposed of their surplus tobacco by smuggling it out, and colonial merchants compensated for their lack of access to the world market by buying goods from the pirates.

The illicit complicity between the American colonies and the pirates was widespread by the 1690s. With few exceptions, colonial governors from New England to the Carolinas colluded with the pirates. Boston, New York, and Philadelphia became pirate depots. In fact, the Pennsylvania surveyor of customs reported that the pirates were so brazen in their activities as to have believed themselves almost beyond reproach:

> They walk the streets with their pockets full of gold and are the constant companion of the [heads of] the Government. They threaten my life and those who were active in apprehending them; carry their profitable goods publicly in boats from one place to another for a market; threaten the lives of the King's [tax] collectors and with force and arms rescue the goods from them. All these parts swarm with pirates, so that if some speedy and effectual course be not taken the trade of America will be ruined.

Piracy, for whatever reason a man might adopt it as a lifestyle, was hardly an upwardly mobile career choice. With the many risks a pirate faced, such as dying in battle, contracting one of the rampant diseases that plagued seamen of the era, or ending up swinging from the end of a rope, the life expectancy of a man once he became a pirate was a mere three to five years. So why would any person in his right mind choose such a way of life? The answers were probably as varied as the pirates themselves, but a distillation of the facts provides two simple explanations that may have accounted for the majority. First, some people simply seem destined for a life of crime and violence. Though the chances of adopting a criminal lifestyle are certainly greater for people from rough backgrounds, sometimes those who grew up with all the advantages still turn to crime. Second, injustices were rampant in seventeenth- and eighteenth-century society. Conditions in the western world's navies were extremely harsh, and some men who had been pressed into service may have turned to piracy after serving under captains who doled out floggings too liberally. Even small infractions of the law could lead to lengthy stays in dungeonlike prisons with virtually no hope of social redemption. For the poor, who were most likely to suffer the injustices of this system, an escape to the sea and piracy might have been the only way out of a dead-end life. The rules that governed most pirate ships were far fairer than those that governed society at large in that era.

Whatever the reasons a man might have turned to piracy, he soon found himself among a loose-knit band of desperate men whose lives were short, brutish, and cruel. The stories in this book make no attempt to romanticize the life of a pirate. Some of the men began life as villains and died the same way. Others started out with good intentions and simply went astray. Still others considered themselves patriots and enjoyed the good wishes and support of their countries and neighbors—at least those who were on the same side as they were.

The individuals you will meet in the following pages practiced their illegal trade over the course of more than a century, but all shared certain traits. All of these characters were real people whose lives and deeds are recounted here according to the best historical records available, and all of their exploits and adventures were intertwined with the long, intricate, and rich history of the coastline of Virginia, whose inlets and rivers once teemed with black flags and frightened cries of "Pirates to starboard; man the guns!"

We hope you enjoy this book and wish you smooth sailing and safe harbors.

William Claiborne

In 1607, the first English colony in North America was established at Jamestown, Virginia. Sadly, things did not go well for the colonists. Captain John Smith and the rest of the settlers almost immediately began to succumb to disease and starvation, and relations with the indigenous tribes of the Virginia coastline were hostile. If the British Crown wanted to maintain a foothold in the New World, then England needed to send support and relief in order for the Jamestown colony to survive. In response to the crisis, nine large ships loaded with settlers and supplies left England for Jamestown in 1609. They arrived on May 24, 1610, to find that only 60 of the original 104 settlers were still living. They abandoned Jamestown and sought locations for new settlements.

While the British fretted over Jamestown, Spain grew increasingly worried. For decades, the Spanish had held complete control over trade with the Western Hemisphere. The Spanish ambassador in England, Pedro de Zuniga, sent a frantic message to his king, Philip III, stating, "I believe that they [England] would again send people out, because, no doubt, the reason they want that place is its apparent suitability for piracy." His fears were well founded. Multiple locations along the American coastline could be used to launch pirate raids on lucrative Spanish shipping vessels, which had always crossed the Atlantic virtually unchallenged. Suggestions were even made in the British Parliament that hundreds of Irish pirates who had been plaguing English shipping could be deported to Virginia to settle, establish colonies, and use their seaborne trade to pillage Spanish vessels.

In 1621, Sir Francis Wyatt arrived in the Chesapeake Bay region to assume command as governor of Virginia. Over the preceding decade, the colony had evolved to a reasonably well-ordered and prosperous state. In all, more than thirteen hundred settlers had arrived in the colony, where they set about clearing land for farmsteads and building new homes. They had finally established peaceful relations with the local Indian tribes, imminent starvation no longer threatened, the menace of possible Spanish intervention had subsided, and a crop of tobacco grown for export was thriving.

One of those who had sailed for Virginia on the same ship as future governor Sir Francis Wyatt was a thirty-four-year-old stockholder in the Virginia Company, a well-educated, hearty, and affable but pugnacious man named William Claiborne. Claiborne had been a friend of Captain John Smith's back in London and through political connections had secured a three-year appointment as the colony's land surveyor. Claiborne had courage, industry, and resolve, but little could he imagine as he was sailing toward the Virginia Capes that he would one day be branded a pirate. Nor could he have foreseen the turmoil that his personal enterprises would inflict on the political geography and future of the entire Tidewater region.

William Claiborne had become good friends with the new governor on the transatlantic crossing and rose rapidly through the ranks of the Virginia colony's governing council. By 1624, he was a valued and trusted member of the governor's council, and in 1626, he became secretary of state for Virginia. Claiborne acquired massive tracts of land, but he sought to expand his holdings, as well as those of Virginia, by exploring the head of the Chesapeake River and any parts of Virginia lying between latitudes 34 and 41 degrees north. He also hoped to establish further trade relations with the Indians.

The seaborne leg of Claiborne's expedition began on April 27, 1627, when he sailed northward along the rich and unsettled shorelines of the Chesapeake. It was during this exploratory voyage that Claiborne first sighted the fertile fields and forests of a large island. Perhaps because it reminded him of his native county of Kent, England, he named it Kent Island. He envisioned this as the perfect base from which to establish an Indian fur-trading empire. The island was nearly three-quarters of the way up the bay—close enough to the mouth of the Susquehanna River to have access to the northern tribes, yet within several days of Jamestown by water. By 1628, Claiborne was actively trading with the Indians and laying the foundations of a successful enterprise.

Less than three years later, with his commission as surveyor complete, Claiborne returned to England to secure financial support for a major trading operation on the Chesapeake. Apparently it did not take much to persuade a wealthy and influential London merchant named William Cloberry to invest heavily in Claiborne's fur-trading enterprise. Cloberry founded a new trading company, of which Claiborne was a partner and independent manager. While in London, Claiborne learned of a new colonizing effort being spearheaded by George Calvert, Lord Baltimore, who sought to stake out a portion of the New World as a Catholic stronghold. This would have been of little interest to Claiborne were it not for the fact that Lord Baltimore had his eyes set on a large expanse of coastal land immediately to the north of Virginia—too close for comfort to Claiborne's burgeoning trading empire. Storm clouds were gathering on the Virginia-Maryland horizon.

Using Cloberry's influential connections, Claiborne managed to acquire a royal license "to trade and traffic of corne, furs, or any other commodities . . . make discoveries for increase of trade" and "freely conduct said trade with his ships, men, boats and merchandise . . . in all parts of America for which there is not already a patent granted to others for trade." Claiborne immediately set sail from Kent, England, aboard a ship named *Africa*, with a cargo of trade goods valued at more than 1,300 pounds sterling and about twenty indentured servants. They landed at Kecoughtan, Virginia, two months later.

At the time of his return, the island at the center of his plans was "unplanted by any man, but possessed of the natives of that country." Claiborne purchased the island from the Indians and then proceeded to develop the land, putting a hundred men to work building homes and mills, laying out gardens, planting orchards, and stocking farms with cattle. Within a year, the island had its own representative in the Virginia Assembly.

Meanwhile, as William Claiborne systematically established a base for his new trading empire on the Chesapeake, Lord Baltimore continued pressing the British king, Charles I, for a charter to establish his new colony north of Virginia. The colony was to be named Maryland in honor of Queen Henrietta Marie. Lord Baltimore died in April 1632, but his efforts were not in vain. The king agreed to the charter in June, which was then granted to Calvert's eldest son, Cecilius, Second Lord Baltimore.

Unfortunately, the territorial borders assigned to the proposed Maryland colony significantly overlapped areas that had been granted to the Virginia Company and were claimed by the colony of Virginia. To make matters worse, Claiborne's Kent Island lay in the middle of the territory claimed by both Virginia and the proposed colony of Maryland. Aware of Claiborne's trading settlement, the new Lord Baltimore initially took a conciliatory stance toward the Virginia secretary of state's claim. He gave instructions that his brother Leonard Calvert—who would become the future governor of the Maryland colony—deal firmly but courteously with Claiborne. It was made clear that Lord Baltimore believed that Kent Island lay fully within the boundaries of the Maryland charter, and while they would permit Claiborne to continue trading, it would have to be under license and authority of Lord Baltimore.

Once word of Baltimore's charter arrived in Virginia, the colony's planters were enraged over the challenge to their established borders. They immediately petitioned the king to redress the issue. The king, however, decided to leave the colonists sort out the problem among themselves. It was a decision that would, in short order, result in charges of piracy, bloodshed, and the first naval engagement between English-speaking peoples in the New World.

Two small vessels carrying the first settlers for young Lord Baltimore's new colony arrived within sight of Point Comfort in the Chesapeake River on February 27, 1634. It was a dangerous landfall, as Baltimore had specifically forbade entry at either Jamestown or Virginia's new fort at Point Comfort.

The Maryland colonists, however, were treated kindly by Virginia's governor, John Harvey, despite the outright hostility of the Virginia Council. Governor Harvey seemed eager to lay aside the challenge to Virginia's territorial jurisdiction and assist the Maryland colonists. As a practiced politician, he obviously was motivated more out of a desire for personal gain than simple neighborliness. It seems that Harvey had made an arrangement with Lord Baltimore to assist the colonists, and in exchange he would "receive a great summe of money due to him out of the exchequer."

After meeting with Maryland's future governor, Leonard Calvert, William Claiborne requested the Virginia Council's opinion as to "how he should demean himself in respect to Lord Baltimore's patent and his deputies, now seated in the bay; for that they [the Marylanders] had specified . . . that he was now a member of that plantation, and therefore should relinquish all relations and dependence on this colony." The council—in opposition, perhaps, to the will of their own governor—stoutly reassured him that Kent Island remained part of the Virginia colony.

Each colony now seemed equally adamant in its claim to the island, so Claiborne decided to take matters into his own hands. Though he had served as both the secretary of state for the colony of Virginia and a member of the Virginia Council, he decided to oppose the king's charter and resist the authority that Lord Baltimore claimed over Kent Island. It was with this decision that Claiborne's real troubles began.

Leonard Calvert's band of colonists began establishing the settlement of St. Mary's City on a bluff overlooking a tributary of the Potomac that they dubbed St. Mary's River. They initially secured the friendship of the local Algonquin Indians, but by the summer of 1643, suspicion, distrust, and periodic hostilities were increasingly evident among the neighboring Patuxent tribe. Alarmed by this change in local attitude to their presence, the settlers of St Mary's abandoned their domestic projects and set about building defenses. A Virginia fur trader named Henry Fleet informed the Maryland colonists that none other than William Claiborne was spreading a rumor among the Indians that the new settlers were "Waspaines," or Spaniards intent on murdering the local tribes.

The Maryland settlers were outraged and immediately made a formal complaint to Virginia governor John Harvey, who had Claiborne placed under bond and confined to Jamestown under the watchful custody of Captains Samuel Matthews and John Utie until the charges could be investigated. On June 20, 1634, commissioners from both Maryland and Virginia, along with Claiborne, met with the Indians at their village on the Patuxent River. As a consequence of the meeting, not only was William Claiborne fully vindicated of the charge of turning the Indians against the Marylanders, but it also became apparent that Henry Fleet had started the rumor because he was jealous of Claiborne's success in the fur-trading business.

Meanwhile, Claiborne's partners, William Cloberry and Company, had petitioned the king of England for protection of their claims on Kent Island. The king replied that it was contrary to justice and the intent of the colonial charter granted to the Calverts that the Kent Islanders be dispossessed. Furthermore, he directed that they should continue to enjoy full freedom of trade and instructed Lord Baltimore not to disturb or molest the island settlement in any way.

That should have been the end of it, but it wasn't. In September, news of the king's command and the charges against Claiborne both reached Lord Baltimore—but not the news that Claiborne had been exonerated of all charges. Based on this incomplete information, Baltimore became outraged. Ignoring the king's admonition to the contrary, he sent word to his brother, Governor Calvert, that if Claiborne continued to trade without an official Maryland license, he was to be arrested and held in St. Mary's jail, and his island settlement was to be confiscated. But arresting the secretary of state of a more powerful and better-established neighboring colony was not a simple matter. So Lord Baltimore used his connections at court to bring pressure on Virginia's governor to promise full support to Maryland in its claims. Opposition to both Governor Harvey and the Maryland colony was spreading throughout Virginia, and trade and commerce between the two colonies now virtually ceased.

William Claiborne resolved to stand fast, in spite of his own governor's support of Lord Baltimore. He prepared Kent Island for armed resistance while simultaneously expanding operations on the island. He imported more servants, cleared more land, and erected more houses. And his partner, William Cloberry, reassured by the king's support, sent new shiploads of goods to trade with the Indians.

When the Europeans' squabbling over Kent Island became unbearable to the indigenous Indians, the island became the target of a raid by hostile Susquehannock and Wicomese tribes, who killed three of the islanders before being repelled. After the attack, the islanders erected two more fortifications as defense against enemies both foreign and domestic. As part of his overall plan, Claiborne had also commissioned the construction of a lightweight ship, known as a "pinnace." Named the *Long Tayle*, it had been designed for naval defense as well as trade and transport. Once complete, Claiborne put the *Long Tayle* and her crew of twenty men under the command of Captain Thomas Smith.

The flashpoint for the escalating hostilities between the St. Mary's and Kent Island camps came when another pinnace belonging to Maryland, commanded by Sergeant Robert Vaughn, approached Garrett Island near the head of the Chesapeake with a large cargo destined for the Indian trade. The historical record is unclear as to how the altercation started or exactly what transpired, but a man named John Butler, agent for and brother-in-law of William Claiborne, seized the Maryland ship, its cargo, Sergeant Vaughn, and the rest of the crew. The prisoners were taken to Kent Island. This seizure became the first documented act of "Pyracie" on the waters of the Chesapeake Bay.

Claiborne quickly ordered the Marylanders released, but with the understanding that they would carry word back to St. Mary's of his resolve to resist any incursion on the part of the Marylanders. He then continued in his trading activities as though nothing had happened. On April 5, Captain Smith sailed the *Long Tayle* on a trading mission to the Indian village at Mattapany, on the shores of the Patuxent River in St. Mary's County. In retaliation for the earlier capture, Captains Fleet and Humber seized the *Long Tayle* and ordered Captain Smith to produce a valid trading license from Lord Baltimore. Smith could not produce the demanded license, but he did produce a copy of the king's commission and additional correspondence confirming it. The Marylanders declared the documents false and proceeded to confiscate the vessel and its cargo. They did, however, release Captain Smith. Apparently, they wanted it well known that Maryland would not tolerate any incursion into its territory.

The Kent Islanders were enraged by the capture of their only ship and sought revenge. They fitted out and armed a sloop named the *Cockatrice*, manning it with a crew of fourteen. Claiborne issued a special warrant to Lieutenant Ratcliffe Warren to seize any vessel belonging to Maryland. It was a warrant that was—depending on one's point of view—either a declaration of war or a letter of marque for privateering. Governor Calvert, fearing the escalating vendetta, armed and readied two vessels of his own, the *St. Helen* and *St. Margaret* and placed them under the command of his most trusted officers, Captain Thomas Cornwaleys and Cuthbert Fenwick.

Just over two weeks after the confiscation of the *Long Tayle*, while cruising in the Pocomoke River on Virginia's lower eastern shore, Lieutenant Warren sighted the *St. Helen* and moved to take the ship. Just as the *Cockatrice* cruised into range, its crew was surprised by the arrival of the *St. Margaret*, commanded by Captain Cornwaleys. Undaunted, the Kent Islanders shifted direction, closed, and attempted to board the *St. Margaret*. A short, brutal hand-to-hand battle ensued, resulting in the deaths of Warren as well as two other Kent Islanders and one member of the *St. Margaret*'s crew. Several more crewmen on both sides were wounded, and the *Cockatrice* was captured. The first blood of naval combat on the Chesapeake Bay had been spilled. It would be far from the last.

For William Claiborne, the loss of the *Cockatrice* was devastating, but he promptly dispatched another armed vessel under the command of Captain Thomas Smith to patrol the mouth of the Pocomoke. On May 10, Smith encountered Cornwaleys and his ship in the harbor of the Great Wicomico. Though the details of the ensuing engagement were never recorded, the Kent Islanders apparently emerged victorious as Cornwaleys's corn, furs, trading goods, and possibly his ship were captured. They had settled the score for the loss and capture of the *Cockatrice*. Claiborne next sent Captain Philip Taylor in another vessel up the Patuxent to retake the *Long Tayle*, but once again the tables turned, and this time Captain Taylor was taken.

While his "privateers" were waging recurring battles on the Pocomoke, Claiborne was at Jamestown garnering support against Governor Harvey. Governor Calvert of Maryland, having failed to capture Claiborne, demanded that the Virginia governor surrender the pirate for trial in Maryland, but Harvey had been growing increasingly unpopular and was now facing open insurrection because of his support for the Marylanders' claim against the Kent Islanders. As a result of his problems at home, Harvey was unable to comply with the demands of his northern neighbors. In fact, Harvey was impeached and sent to England to face charges. In his place, the Virginia Council elected Captain John West as acting governor, and forged an uneasy truce between the Marylanders at St. Mary's and the Kent Islanders.

Next George Evelin arrived on the scene. When Evelin came to Kent Island in December 1636 with a one-sixth share in Cloberry and Company, he seemed a welcome asset. But when the first shipment of supplies, trade goods, and servants arrived a couple months later, the islanders learned that Evelin had somehow managed to acquire power of attorney through Cloberry, and now he declared that he had been granted command of Kent Island and full control of all its operations. William Claiborne was ordered to return to England to explain his actions against Lord Baltimore. Claiborne dutifully made preparations for his transatlantic voyage, but before he left, he made rapid progress on a permanent plantation and trading center under the command of Captain Thomas Smith on Palmer's Island, strategically located at the head of the bay and in the heart of Maryland territory. He also prepared an inventory of company property and made Evelin sign a bond agreeing not to sell or assign away Kent Island or its goods.

As soon as Claiborne disappeared over the eastern horizon, however, Evelin broke the bond and began personal negotiations with Maryland's governor. Courted, flattered, and likely bribed by the clever Governor Calvert, Evelin soon transferred his allegiance from Cloberry and Company to Lord Baltimore. Calvert instructed him to secure the goodwill of the Kent Islanders in support of Lord Baltimore, and in exchange, the governor would appoint him as commander of Kent Island, from which he would receive a share in all proceeds.

The Kent Islanders, however, viewing Evelin as both a traitor and a turncoat, were loath to transfer their allegiance to Lord Baltimore, despite the best efforts of their new commander. Trade deteriorated and the Marylanders severed the supply lines. The threat of starvation was growing among the islanders, who almost universally despised Evelin. Two of Claiborne's most trusted and loyal agents, John Butler and Thomas Smith, led the islanders in resistance against the usurper Evelin and soon became marked men among Maryland's officers.

Governor Calvert, whose past forays against the Kent Islanders had not fared well, was reluctant to employ force of arms to reinstall Evelin to command without clear instructions from his brother, Lord Baltimore, who remained safely back in England. In the late autumn of 1637, however, news reached the Marylanders that a possible attack on the colony by Susquehannock Indians was likely. Maryland feared that the Virginians might supply the Indians with guns and powder via the trading post at Palmer's Island. They decided, therefore, that both Kent and Palmer's Islands would have to be taken by force. Calvert immediately set about gathering a force of roughly thirty musketeers under the command of Cornwaleys, which moved out with George Evelin in tow. Meanwhile, the Kent Islanders had heard about the Marylanders' fear of an Indian attack and decided it might actually be a good idea to supply and encourage the Susquehannocks while simultaneously fortifying Palmer's Island.

The Marylanders landed at the southernmost point of Kent Island a little before sunset near Captain Claiborne's house, which was "seated within a small fort of Pallysadoes." The Marylanders took the lightly defended fort by surprise and without opposition. Claiborne was still in England, and a thorough search failed to turn up Butler or Smith, "the chief incendiaries of the former seditions and mutinies upon the island." Undeterred, Governor Calvert rounded up everyone in the fort and set off on a march toward Butler's plantation five miles to the north. He directed his ship to rendezvous with them at Craford, Evelin's headquarters on the island. When the Marylanders came within half a mile of Butler's plantation, Calvert dispatched an ensign named Clerck with ten musketeers to surprise and capture Butler and bring him to Craford. He next dispatched his sergeant, Robert Vaughn, along with six musketeers to Thomas Smith's plantation at Beaver Neck, located on the far side of a small creek. They captured both Butler and Smith, who put up little resistance, and confined them aboard the pinnace on charges of piracy.

Having thus captured the leaders of the opposition, Governor Calvert issued a proclamation of general pardon to any remaining Kent Islanders who submitted to Lord Baltimore's government within twenty-four hours. Not surprisingly, this is precisely what all the residents of Kent Island did. Calvert then directed that the islanders would have to accept Lord Baltimore's letters patent for their holdings on the island, telling them that new boundaries would be surveyed in the spring. Happy with the outcome of his mission, Calvert sailed back to St Mary's with Smith and Butler under heavy guard, leaving George Evelin firmly in command of Kent Island.

Once he arrived at St. Mary's, Calvert faced the vexing question of what to do with Butler and Smith. In an effort to win him over to Lord

Baltimore's side, Calvert brought Butler out of the sheriff's custody and into his own home. If he could somehow manage to successfully secure the influential Butler's support, he hoped the rest of Kent Island might follow suit. Smith, on the other hand, had commanded two of Claiborne's ships and was responsible for the death of William Ashmore at the Battle of Pocomoke, as it had come to be called. Calvert needed to make an example of Smith and could not treat him as generously as he had Butler, so in March 1638, Smith was indicted, found guilty, and sentenced to be hanged for piracy and murder.

As a show of mercy and clemency, however, Governor Calvert issued a stay of execution and released Smith on bail, hoping he had made his point and duly demonstrated his power and authority. Now free on bail, Smith returned to Kent Island, where he immediately set about raising a revolt against Maryland.

Calvert fitted out a second expedition and returned to the troublesome island with fifty musketeers. They reinforced the Kent Island fort with several cannons and removed all of Cloberry's goods and servants. The Marylanders once again captured Smith and took him to St. Mary's under guard. This time, though, there would be no mercy. He was hanged—not for piracy, but for rebellion.

Butler eventually converted to the Maryland cause and was appointed captain of the Militia Band of the Isle of Kent. Ironically, his commission included mustering inhabitants capable of bearing arms to repel pirate invasions and Indians, as well as suppressing mutiny and civil disorder.

Meanwhile, Captain William Claiborne, whom the Maryland Assembly charged on March 24, 1638, with "grevious crimes of pyracie and murther" for the Battle of Pocomoke, became a wanted criminal and outlaw in the Maryland colony. Consequently, he forfeited all of "his lands and tenements" as well as his "goods and chattels which he hath within this Province" to Lord Baltimore.

Naturally, Claiborne petitioned the king. The Crown, however, wanted nothing more to do with the quarrelsome colonies and referred the matter to the Lords Commissioners of Plantations. Fortune continued to frown on the former Virginia secretary of state, as in April 1638, the Lords Commissioners predictably ruled in favor of their peer, Lord Baltimore. Baltimore's power and influence in England was simply too great to fight.

With such powerful political forces in England standing firmly behind Maryland, and with both Kent and Palmer's Islands firmly under the control of Governor Calvert, the newly elected governor of Virginia withdrew all support from William Claiborne. He was ruined. And the islands became a permanent part of Maryland.

William
Dampier

"I may without vanity encourage the reader to expect many things wholly new."

Nearly everything we know about William Dampier's early life is what he tells us in the first chapter of his *Voyages to the Bay of Campeachy*. According to Dampier, he was born in the first half of 1652 to a farming family living in East Coker, near Yeovil in Somerset County, England. His parents hoped William would go into commerce and sent him to school, where he attended Latin class. His father died in 1662 and his mother in 1668. After his mother's death, his guardians removed him from the Latin school in favor of instruction in writing and arithmetic, giving him more modern, practical commercial skills. A year or so later, having had "very early inclinations to see the world," he became an apprentice to the master of a ship out of the port of Weymouth and traveled to France and then Newfoundland. He was "pinched with the rigour of that cold climate," he wrote, and set his heart on a long voyage to more summery seas. His chance at a warm-weather cruise came when, at age nineteen, he set off for Bantam in Indonesia. After returning home in early 1672, he spent the rest of his twentieth year with his brother in Somersetshire.

Dampier never quite adapted to life back on land, and a year later, he enlisted in the Royal Navy and fought in the Third Anglo-Dutch War. His first two engagements were on the *Prince Royal* under Sir Edward Spragge. A day or two before Spragge's third battle, in which Sir Edward was killed, Dampier fell sick and was sent ashore. After a long illness, he went home to his brother. During his convalescence, a neighbor named Colonel Hillier offered him a job helping manage his plantation in Jamaica under the overseer, a Mr. Whalley. Dampier was anxious to travel again and soon set sail on the *Content of London*, earning his passage by working as a common seaman.

He worked with Whalley on the oddly named 16-Mile Walk plantation for six months, and then left to work for a Captain Heming, who owned a plantation at St. Ann's, on the north end of the island. Evidently life on land simply did not suit William Dampier, and he quit this second job, writing that he was clearly out of his element. He then spent several months working on trading ships that cruised around the island. On these trips, he "[be]came acquainted with all the ports and bays about Jamaica and with their manufactures, as also with the benefit of the land and sea-winds." He also began keeping the journals from which our knowledge of his life and adventures comes.

Always willing to try something new, Dampier spent about two years between 1675 and 1678 cutting and loading logwood on the Spanish-owned Bay of Campeche at the southern tip of the Gulf of Mexico. Dampier believed at least 270 Englishmen were engaged in the logwood trade, and the Spanish were unable to stop this foreign intrusion into their territory. "It is not my business," he said, "to determine how far we might have a right of cutting wood there." Dampier enjoyed the work but was unable to make much money at it, so he eventually decided to sail with some privateers running in the southern reaches of the Gulf of Mexico.

He returned to London in August 1678 and allowed himself only a six-month leave. Making the most of his time ashore, he married a woman named Judith, who worked for the Duke of Grafton. There is no record that they had any children, and nothing more is known of his poor wife until some twenty-five years later. Running out of money and anxious to get back to sea, Dampier planned another expedition to Campeche but, as he described it in his journal, the trip "proved to be a voyage round the world."

In early 1679, Dampier embarked as a passenger on the *Loyal Merchant of London*, which arrived in Jamaica in April, and he spent the remainder of the year there. He must have made a fair profit from the trip, because he bought a small estate in Dorsetshire, back in England. He was about to return home to complete the purchase when a Mr.

Hobby invited him to join in a trading voyage to the Mosquito Coast, off what are now Nicaragua and Honduras. Dampier was eager to accept, so he sent the money to buy his estate back to England with a friend, while he set sail with Hobby. By a strange twist of fate, Hobby's ship landed at Negril Bay, at the west end of Jamaica, where a squadron of buccaneers was assembled under Captains Coxon, Sawkins, and Bartholomew Sharp. The temptation that led many honest men into the buccaneering life seized nearly the entire crew of Hobby's ship. According to Dampier, "Mr. Hobby's men all left him to go with them upon an expedition they had contrived, leaving not one with him beside myself." After three or four days, Dampier also succumbed to temptation and joined the pirates, leaving poor Mr. Hobby stranded in Negril Bay.

Dampier joined the group of pirates led by Captain Bartholomew Sharp, who commanded an impressive flotilla of about twelve ships. Although England was at peace with Spain, this did not stop the pirates from raiding more than twenty-five Spanish ships and attacking the Spanish-owned town of Portobello, Panama.

Naturally, the Spanish were unhappy with the raids and tried to apprehend the pirates, but Sharp eluded them by splitting up his ships. The Spanish assumed that Britain would deal with the pirates, but the Crown had little motivation to protect Spanish interests, particularly when the pirates proved they really were buccaneers and shared at least some of their takings with the English government. It seems that one of the Spanish ships that Sharp and his men, including Dampier, took was the *San Rosario*, which carried, in addition to large quantities of wine, gunpowder, and gold, a book of detailed charts and maps of the South Seas. These were of such strategic importance that when the pirates returned to England, they presented them to Charles II, who granted the crew a full pardon.

The pirates' next expedition revolved around an attack on the city of Portobello, Panama. With an impressive force of nine ships, including seven English and two French privateer ships and a total of 477 men, they easily took Portobello. Although another pirate, Henry Morgan, had sacked the city only eleven years earlier, each of the men received 40 pounds sterling in booty. After the sack of Portobello, a group of friendly Indians volunteered to lead the pirates on a march across the Isthmus of Panama to the city of Santa Maria. The two French crews refused to take part in the plan, insisting that they had no intention of marching across Panama. Two of the captains remained behind with a skeleton crew to guard the ships, while an expeditionary force of 331 men rowed ashore and marched forward in seven companies.

For ten days, they marched through the tropical nightmare of the Panamanian jungle, and although they took Santa Maria without losing a single man, they came away virtually empty-handed. Angry and frustrated, the pirates headed back to their ships but became separated along the way. One party of only sixty-eight men reached the shore near the island of Perico, where they found five huge ships and three fairly large barks floating at anchor. They used five canoes they had borrowed from the Indians to attack the barks, taking them after a desperate resistance by their crews. In the furious battle, a Spanish admiral was killed and one of the barks lost sixty-one out of eighty-six men; all but eight of the rest were wounded. The buccaneers' casualties were eighteen killed and twenty-two wounded. Only when the smoke cleared did the pirates discover that the five largest ships were completely deserted, their crews having been transferred to the barks. The victorious pirates claimed the biggest of the ships, the four hundred-ton *La Santissima Trinidad*. It was a mighty victory, but its heavy cost caused serious friction among the remaining pirates.

Captain Coxon, the commander in chief of the pirate band, was charged with holding back during the engagement, and some of the men "brand[ed] him with the note of cowardice." Coxon withdrew his ship from the fleet, taking seventy men with him, but the seeds of dissent had been sown. Things only got worse after their next attack, on the town of Puebla Nova, was a total failure that cost the life of Captain Sawkins, the new and highly popular commander of the pirate force. Sixty-three men who were particularly loyal to the late Captain Sawkins mutinied and sailed away. They had barely left when another mutiny broke out among the remaining men. The men on one of the prizes assigned to Captain Edmund Cook refused to serve under him. Cook then joined Sharp's ship, and Captain Cox took over the command of the mutinous crew. The once strong pirate army was slowly dissolving.

The remaining men now turned their attention to the beautiful garden city of La Serena. Although the city had enough wealth to support seven large churches, it refused to pay the ransom of ninety-five thousand pieces of eight the pirates demanded. In retaliation, the pirates burned the city to the ground.

Shortly after this disastrous encounter, yet another mutiny broke out when some of the pirates demanded to go home while others insisted on another cruise up the Pacific coast of South America. In January 1681, Sharp was deposed from his command and replaced by Captain Watling, but the crews remained in smoldering discontent. Watling seems to have thought the best chance of placating the men lay in carrying out a successful coup, and he proposed an attack on the port city of Arica, the port from which was "fetched all the plate [silver] that is carried to Lima, the head city of Peru." In a disastrously disorganized attack, the men stormed the town with reckless courage, and Captain Watling, both quartermasters, and twenty-six of the crew were killed, and eighteen others were desperately wounded. To make matters worse, some, including three surgeons who were drinking instead of fighting or attending to the wounded, were taken prisoners. The Spaniards, who had superior numbers and far greater organization, counterattacked again and again, finally driving the marauders back to their ships.

Captain Sharp resumed command after Watling's death, and although Sharp had often been described as "a man of undaunted courage and of an excellent conduct," many of the men were "not satisfied either with his courage or behaviour," so they put the question of his fitness to a vote. The majority went for Sharp, but a minority of forty-four, including Dampier, seceded from Sharp's command "and chose to go back to the Isthmus rather than stay under a captain in whom [they] experienced neither courage nor [good] conduct."

The following year, 1683, Dampier met a Captain John Cook (not to be confused with the eighteenth-century explorer Captain James Cook) in Virginia. In August, Captain Cook sailed his ship, the *Revenge*, from Accomack, Virginia, to the South Seas, taking with him a seasoned company of seventy hardened veteran privateers. Cook's quartermaster and second in command had been Edward Davis, and his surgeon was Lionel Wafer. All three men had already spent years in the West Indies and the South Seas, roving and raiding under the command of such notable buccaneers as Captains Sharp, Coxton, Wright, and Yanky. They had attacked and taken towns and ships, crossed the sweltering jungles of the Isthmus of Panama on foot, befriended savages in the jungles, and successfully plundered the Spanish town of Tierre Firme.

John Cook was a native "cirole" (today called Creole, people of mixed French and Spanish descent) of the West Indies island of St. Christophers, now known as St. Kitts. His peers saw him as a "sensible man" who had spent the better part of his life at sea as a privateer. Cook rose to prominence first as quartermaster under a Dutch privateer captain named Yanky, and then to captaincy of one of Yanky's prizes captured near the island of Tortuga. When Cook assumed command of this ship, he was accompanied by several other members of Yanky's crew, including longtime friend and companion Edward Davis. Davis and Cook were taken prisoner during an attack by French pirates, but they managed to escape, recapture their ship, and turn the tables by capturing a French merchant ship carrying a cargo of wine.

The crewmen discussed what course they should follow next. They agreed that after reprovisioning and refitting their appropriately named *Revenge* in Virginia, they would cruise through the perilous Straits of Magellan to the South Pacific on the coast of Chile and Peru. In Virginia, many of Captain Wright's company, who had arrived the preceding year, now joined Cook and Davis. One of these was a particularly intelligent, if somewhat serious-looking, diarist and adventurer: the now-thirty-one-year-old William Dampier.

The Eastern Shore of Virginia served the pirates well as a base for refitting their vessels, taking on supplies, and preparing for the dangerous voyage south and around Cape Horn. When Cook, Davis, and their men departed from Virginia, they were sailing into the largely unknown waters of the southern Pacific, barely visited and hardly charted, embarking on what turned out to be a piratical voyage without equal.

They worked their way down the east side of the Americas to the Falkland Islands, pausing only long enough to capture a Spanish ship, transferring their gear to it and renaming it the *Batchelor's Delight*. They steered around Cape Horn to the Juan Fernandez Islands. Here they met another English pirate vessel, called the *Nicholas*, in whose company they sailed up the coasts of Chile and Peru to the Galapagos Islands and then Mexico.

Cook died in Mexico, and Edward Davis took his place. Lionel Wafer, the surgeon, later joined them there. Wafer had been severely injured by an explosion of gunpowder during the transit. The main group left him behind with other stragglers in the charge of friendly local Cuna Indians, with whom he remained for some five months. Wafer, by reason of his medical skill, lived with the Indians "in great splendour and repute." His hosts so adored him that they tattooed him "in yellow, red, and blue, very bright and lovely." When he rejoined his friends at La Sound's Key, he was virtually unrecognizable.

In chronicling these amazing adventures in which he took part, Dampier was so reticent about himself that it is almost impossible to hazard an opinion as to what part he might have taken in any of the buccaneering cruises. He recorded virtually no personal information, not mentioning his rank or what part he took in affairs. Through all of his voyages, he never commanded a ship or an expedition. Apparently he did occasionally give advice, and we know that he joined in the mutiny against Sharp, but he seems to have taken no active part in it. His attitude toward the violent, unpredictable men with whom he served was one of aloofness. His chief concern was not piracy or profit, but rather the study of geography, the winds and tides, the plants and animals, and keeping his journal up-to-date.

While Dampier watched and wrote, the pirates with whom he traveled met up with Captain Charles Swan, commanding the appropriately named *Cygnet*, and they joined forces during 1685. Together, the three pirate ships—Swan's ship and the two commanded by Davis—attacked Spanish ships off the coasts of Panama and Mexico.

The climax of this cruise was to have been the capture of a Spanish fleet carrying treasure from Lima to Panama. By May 1685, two pirates named Captains Townley and Harris, as well as a French contingent under a Captain Gronet, had joined Davis and Swan. The growth in the scope and scale of this pirate movement can be seen in the numbers given by Dampier. The buccaneers had six ships and four tenders, carrying no less than 960 men. They had only 52 guns, however, these being in Davis's and Swan's ships. The Spanish fleet, on the other hand, had fourteen vessels, six of them "of good force," with 174 guns in all. Considering that the pirates were outgunned by more than three to one, it should come as no surprise that everything quickly went against them. The Spaniards had the advantage of the wind being with them, and after a running fight around the bay, the assailants were lucky to have escaped.

Davis cruised for some time along the Pacific coast. He then turned south, rounded Cape Horn, and made his way up the Atlantic coast and through the Caribbean to Virginia, where he settled for about three years. He was then arrested for piracy and sent to London for trial but was acquitted. After some years spent partly in London, he returned to Jamaica, and on the outbreak of the War of the Spanish Succession, he joined a privateer in raids on the Spanish gold mines. More on the voyages, fortunes, and misfortunes of Davis, Wafer, and their associate John Hingson appears in the next chapter, on the adventures of the *Batchelor's Delight*.

By the time Davis and Swan parted company, William Dampier had transferred to Swan's crew and now joined them in crossing the Pacific in an attempt to leave buccaneering and return to honest trading. To induce his men to go with him, however, Swan was obliged to dangle the carrot of further piracy that might await them in the East Indies. At the island of Guam, he made no attempt to pursue an Acapulco ship, being "now wholly averse to any hostile action." At Mindanao, the men conducted themselves as traders and were hospitably entertained by the sultan. Although virtually no trade was available in the area, they did consider settling in the idyllic tropical paradise, but six months of lazy idleness at Mindanao led to serious trouble. Swan became brutal and tyrannical toward his men, succumbed to the pleasures of the town, and took long absences from his ship. Yet another mutiny resulted, and the majority of the crew seized the ship, abandoned Swan, and sailed off under a new captain named Read. Curiously, Dampier's conduct in this situation exhibited the same aloofness as on other occasions. He took no part in either the vain attempt to get Swan back aboard his ship or the men's conspiracy. In spite of his better feelings, William Dampier remained a pirate for another eighteen months.

The voyage under Captain Read, from the buccaneering point of view, was a complete failure. Though their "business was to pillage," they took only two prizes, and those were of little account. They did explore vast stretches of sea and land, however, as the ship wandered from Manila to Pulo Condore to Formosa to Celebes to the north coast of Australia and the Nicobars. Here, in the Nicobar Islands in the eastern Indian Ocean, Dampier finally ended his buccaneering career of eight and a half years. The men had become more and more drunken, quarrelsome, and unruly, and Dampier looked for an opportunity to escape from what he called "this mad crew."

Determined to leave piracy and the pirates behind, Dampier, the ship's surgeon, and another Englishman persuaded a few natives to help them escape in a canoe, and together the group slipped away from the ship in the midst of a howling storm. Dampier huddled against the torrent, terrified that the slashing rain would overwhelm the tiny craft. "I made sad reflections on my former life," he wrote, "and looked back with horror and detestation on actions which before I disliked but now I trembled at the remembrance of." Dampier undoubtedly reflected on his time among the drinking, brawling, half-savage pirates as a descent into a life of sin and debauchery. In retrospect, we can be a bit more forgiving, because while his companions were plying their trade as criminals of the sea, Dampier was studiously recording his observations of plant and animal life, island inhabitants, and their governments, religion, manners, and customs.

For the rest of his round-the-world trip Dampier remained primarily an observer of life around him. The first leg of his voyage home (July 1688 to April 1689) took him to the Gulf of Tonquin in what is now Vietnam, then on to Malacca and Fort George. From there he traveled back to Achin and Bencoolen, where he was employed as a gunner in the English fort for five months. Finally, Dampier booked passage on an England-bound ship named the *Defence*. He arrived home in September 1691, twelve and a half years after first leaving England.

Now thirty-nine years old, William Dampier may have seen the world, circumnavigated the globe, and lived among the pirates, but if he had ever dreamed the old buccaneers' dream of chests of treasure and pieces of eight, he would have been sadly disappointed: when he landed, he had virtually nothing of value. Considering everything he had endured and how little he had to show for it, it might have seemed wise if he had settled down, but rest and roots were apparently not in Dampier's nature.

He subsequently traveled—mostly from place to place by ship—while simultaneously writing his book entitled *New Voyage*, which was published in 1697 and became so successful that Dampier was offered a position with the British Customs Office. From time to time, the British Council of Trade and Plantations office consulted him on proposed expeditions and settlements, particularly if they wanted information on local pirate activity.

Dampier refused to rest on his laurels, and in 1698, he successfully submitted to the government proposals for a new voyage of exploration to New Holland—a vast and unknown island continent now called Australia. He was appointed captain of the twenty-one-gun *Roebuck*, his first command, at the age of forty-seven. The expedition went awry from the first, for a variety of causes. His ship was not seaworthy for a long voyage, and Dampier quarreled with his men, especially his lieutenant, Fisher, whom he clapped in irons and handed over as a prisoner to the Portuguese governor at Bahia.

At Shark's Bay, in western Australia, scurvy and a lack of fresh water and provisions finally proved too much for Dampier to deal with, and he decided to head back to England. However, he only got as far as the lonely shores of Ascension Island in the South Atlantic, which lies nearly a thousand miles from the nearest land mass. By sheer luck, Ascension was a regular stop for Royal Navy ships crossing between Africa and South America, and Dampier and his crew were rescued and taken home by way of Barbados.

Unlike the previous time Dampier had returned to England from his travels, he was no longer a celebrity curiosity. Now he was a failed government employee, and as such, he faced criticism, censure, and at the instigation of the lieutenant he had put in irons, a court-martial. The court-martial found Dampier guilty of "very hard and cruel usage towards Lieutenant Fisher," for which the court held there were no grounds. He was fined all of his pay and declared to be "not a fit person to be employed as commander of any of His Majesty's ships."

Understandably unhappy, Dampier left government service to become a privateer in the War of the Spanish Succession, which broke out in 1701. Investors anxious to cash in on the action fitted out two privateer ships, the *St. George* and the *Fame*, and offered Dampier command of the *St. George*. Almost beyond belief, misfortune continued to plague poor William Dampier. The *Fame* deserted the *St. George* even before they left England. Replacing it was another ship captained by a man named Pickering who, as bad luck would have it, died as the ships neared Brazil.

Pickering's successor, Lieutenant Stradling, could not get along with either his own men or Captain Dampier. The failure to take two enemy ships, general dissension, and a near mutiny led Stradling to maroon one of his seamen, Alexander Selkirk, on a tiny island named Juan Fernandez. Selkirk's four-year epic survival story led to his becoming immortalized both as Robinson Crusoe and as Ben Gunn in *Treasure Island*.

While Selkirk was settling in to a life of bare survival, a furious Dampier abandoned Stradling's ship at Tobago. He then got into a quarrel with his own first mate who, along with twenty-one others, mutinied, abandoned the *St. George*, and took off in a captured bark. The heart of the discipline problem may have lain with Dampier, because shortly after his first mate left, so did another junior officer named Funnell, who took thirty-four more men with him. Left with barely thirty men, Dampier transferred his crew to a captured brigantine and abandoned the leaking *St. George*, only to be taken prisoner by the Dutch and thrown into jail. Dampier was eventually released and made his way back to England.

When Dampier returned from his second voyage, a group of merchants from the city of Bristol were organizing a two-ship privateering expedition to the Pacific under Captain Woodes Rogers. Despite his less than sterling record, Dampier was offered the position of pilot. Of all his voyages, this was undoubtedly his happiest. The expedition was lawful and gave him no qualms of conscience; he was free from the cares and responsibilities of supreme command; he served under one of the most competent captains of the time; and his experience and ability as a navigator enabled him to contribute significantly to the success of the venture.

The two vessels were the *Duke* and *Duchess*, and Dampier sailed on the former with Rogers. The list of officers describes him as "William Dampier, Pilot for the South Seas, who had been already three times there and twice round the World." Perhaps having learned from the experience of Dampier's previous ill-equipped expeditions, the merchants supplied the ships liberally with provisions and gear.

It may say something about sea life during the early eighteenth century that despite the detailed planning and massive provisioning of the expedition, a mutiny broke out on the first leg of the journey, between Cork, Ireland, and the Canary Islands. As an experienced captain, Woodes Rogers promptly put it down, sentencing the ringleader to be whipped by a fellow conspirator. The crew was paid regular

wages, which generally kept troubles to a minimum. Equally important was the fact that Rogers was wise enough to share his responsibil-
ity with his officers, and he referred all questions of importance to
committees, Dampier's name being on nearly every list. Thanks to
Woodes Rogers's experience and skill, he maintained discipline and
the expedition captured numerous ships and a mountain of booty
valued at 170,000 pounds sterling. A large share of this not-so-small
fortune went to Woodes Rogers, who used it to rent the Bahama
Islands from the lords proprietors for twenty-one years and made
himself their governor. Unhappily for Dampier, he did not benefit
from this great pile of plunder, because it was not released and distributed by the Crown until after his death.

The cruise under Woodes Rogers was Dampier's last adventure at
sea. In March 1715, three and a half years after returning to England,
William Dampier died at age sixty-three. Unlike most of the men
whose stories fill this book, he was neither a hero nor a villainous
rogue. He seldom took part in any major activity on any of the ships
on which he served. Only during his last voyage is there any record
that his captain sought his advice or that he offered advice without
being asked. He was caught up in countless mutinies but never took
an active part in any of them and chose sides only when the decision
was forced on him. Although he was not an active buccaneer, he
seems to have done his duty by his associates; at any rate, no complaints against him in this respect were recorded. He did his share of
the strenuous labor, whether afloat or ashore, without engaging in the
drinking bouts and quarrels, and all the while he was carefully writing
in his journal day by day.

For all his great—though often disastrous—adventures, William
Dampier was one of life's observers, writing down everything he saw
and all that happened around him. And this is what makes Dampier
significant. Without him and others like him, we would know far less
than we do about the rough, unhappy, and often violent life of the
pirates and buccaneers of the Golden Age of Piracy.

It is difficult to know what to make of Dampier, but an interesting
insight into his character appears in the writer John Evelyn's account
of his dinner with Samuel Pepys on August 6, 1698:

I dined with Mr. Pepys, where was Captain Dampier, who had
been a famous buccaneer . . . and printed a relation of his very
strange adventure, and his observations. He was now going
abroad again by the King's encouragement, who furnished a
ship of 290 tons. He seemed a more modest man than one
would imagine by relation of the crew he had assorted with.
He brought a map of his observations of the course of the
winds in the South Seas, and assured us that the maps hitherto
extant were all false as to the Pacific Sea, which he makes on
the south of the line, that on the north end running by the
coast of Peru being extremely tempestuous.

It seems Evelyn expected to meet a swashbuckler and found instead
a modest, courteous gentleman, whose main concern at the moment
was his objection to calling an ocean "pacific" unless it was actually
peaceful.

Davis, Wafer, and Hingson: Buccaneers of the *Batchelor's Delight*

In June 1688, three men were arrested as they made their way down the Chesapeake Bay in a small boat. Edward Davis, Lionel Wafer, and John Hingson were transporting three chests filled with silver plate and Spanish gold coins. The men claimed innocence, but Peter Cloise, a black slave who belonged to Davis, said they were all pirates and comrades who had sailed together and plundered Spanish towns. So who were these men? How did they end up in a rowboat on the Chesapeake Bay, nearly capsizing under the weight of the treasure they carried? Were they pirates, or were they, in fact, as innocent as they claimed? The historical truth, as is often the case, lies somewhere in between. This is their story.

In 1682, Charles II was regarded by many at the time as the best king England ever had. However, since Charles was ill and had no legitimate heir, his younger brother James was next in line for the throne, and James had a good chance of becoming the worst king England ever had. Trying to avoid a bad situation before it occurred, a group of about fifty men in their early twenties decided to get out of England while the getting was good and seek their fortunes elsewhere. They intended to go on a privateering voyage to the Caribbean, even though they knew little about sailing.

After obtaining letters of marque from King Charles's government, the ad hoc collection of would-be privateers bought an old French ship called the *Revenge*, which another group of privateers had captured in the Caribbean and put up for sale in London, and they hired its previous owner, an experienced captain and privateer named John Cooke, who had commanded an entire pirate fleet only a short time earlier. Cooke declared, through hard-learned experience, that the most important asset for a privateering cruise was a competent ship's doctor. The adventurers and their captain first sailed to the Caribbean, where they picked up Dr. Lionel Wafer (sometimes spelled DelaWafer), ship's "chirurgeon" (surgeon), in Panama. Wafer had served Cooke's fleet of privateers as surgeon in 1679, until he was persuaded to join another group of privateers commanded by Bartholomew Sharp off Cartagena, Colombia.

Captain Sharp and his men had then abandoned Wafer in the jungles of Panama, when the doctor had been seriously wounded in the thigh by the accidental explosion of a keg of gunpowder. The local Cuna Indians had not only saved his life, but also healed the wound thanks to their skill with herbal medicine—skills they had passed on to Wafer. In fact, when Cooke first arrived in Panama, he failed to recognize Wafer because the good doctor had gone native, dressing and painting himself exactly like the Cuna Indians, and having been covered in colorful tattoos. One of Wafer's friends, John Hingson (also spelled both Hinson and Hingsett), had stood by him through his abandonment, recovery, and odd change in fashion sense, so he too was welcomed aboard the *Revenge*.

Wafer and Hingson had heard that another old colleague, William Dampier (whose story is told earlier in this book), was hiding out at Hampton, Virginia, hoping to escape the notice of the authorities after having been involved in some notorious pirate exploits. Also in hiding with Dampier was another old comrade named Edward Davis. Dampier had sailed around the world in 1679, so his expertise was considered crucial to the success of the new voyage. In April 1683, the would-be privateers sailed to Hampton, where they persuaded Dampier and Davis to join them, and on August 23, the group sailed for the Guinea coast of Africa. After a three-month voyage, they arrived off the African coast in late November 1683.

Their ship was hardly new, and the long voyage—from the Caribbean to London and back, then up to Virginia and across the Atlantic to Africa—had taken a heavy toll on the rotting wooden hull. Consequently, Captain Cooke announced that the next order of business was to find a suitable replacement vessel. They spotted a small Danish ship anchored in the Sierra Leone River, presumably waiting for a cargo of slaves. It was smaller than the *Revenge*, but it had the favorable characteristic of being virtually new, freshly launched from the dockyards of Copenhagen.

But slave traders were a hard-bitten lot, and the privateers were smart enough to realize they were as yet untested in battle, so they soon devised a clever plan. Dampier and crewman William Cowley challenged the slavers to an all-night marathon card game, with their ships as the intended stakes. Somehow the fledgling privateers managed to win the game, and they renamed their new ship the *Batchelor's Delight*. Presumably the Danes received the rotting *Revenge* as a consolation prize. One crewmember of the *Batchelor's Delight* later boasted that they had seized the Danish ship by force, that it was loaded with female slaves whom the pirates took as consorts, and that they burned the *Revenge* so as to leave no trace, but the surviving evidence does not support this apparently embellished course of events.

The *Batchelor's Delight* was generally described as pretty, and some reports called her a large frigate of up to forty guns, but other sources, including two pictures of the ship, show her to have been a mere corvette with just fourteen main guns. Another ship during the same time period had a similar name with a slightly different spelling, the *Bachelor's Delight*, which may explain the confusion over the ship's description. The *Bachelor's Delight* sailed from Boston under Captain Benjamin Gillam on a privateering voyage on June 21, 1682, arriving nearly a month later, on August 18, at Nelson River at the southwest corner of Hudson's Bay, in what is now Manitoba, Canada. The crew founded a private fort (later a principal outpost of the Hudson's Bay Company), but the French captured the fort, ship, and men. The ship and crew spent the winter under arrest in Hudson's Bay and sailed to Quebec the following summer. The French authorities released them in October 1683. This is clearly a different ship and is significant only in the confusion it creates for naval historians. But we digress.

Captain Cooke, William Dampier, Edward Davis, and Dr. Wafer decided the Caribbean was not the most suitable place to become a pirate, because it was infested with Spanish military patrols. They were actively suppressing the chief pirate bases at Tortuga and Petit-Goave, Haiti, so it seemed far safer for the privateers to roam along the Pacific coast of Latin America. No roads could be built along that coast because the terrain was nearly vertical from the shoreline to the peaks of the Andes. The Spanish knew it was almost impossible to sail around Cape Horn, so they felt safe in not fortifying their west-coast cities or paying for expensive warships to police the Pacific waters. Consequently, mountains of Spanish silver, gold, and jewels from the mines of the interior moved along the coast in nearly unarmed merchant ships, which ferried the booty northward to Panama.

Accordingly, the English adventurers braved the perilous passage around Cape Horn in their fine new ship, and they spent several years plundering their way from southern Chile up to California. For the pirates, this was a time of exciting adventures, harrowing escapes, and several notable defeats of Spanish warships. The brigands hid among the numerous islands along the coast and became the first Englishmen ever to see the Galapagos. Dampier was the first man to make notes and observations on the wildlife that would be essential to Darwin's work on evolution 150 years later. With the help of William Cowley, Dampier made the first charts of the Galapagos and gave the individual islands their present-day English names. The crewmen of the *Batchelor's Delight* were also the first Europeans to see Easter Island, far off the coast of Chile, although they gave it a different name and did not stop to explore it. Westerners did not see Easter Island again until Easter Sunday 1722.

Captain John Cooke died off Costa Rica in 1684 of a tropical disease picked up in Chile, and the crew voted to replace him with the experienced Edward Davis, Dampier's friend. By this time, several English and French privateer ships were operating along the west coast of Latin America. These were former Spanish merchant ships, captured and armed by disorganized English and French pirates who had trudged across the Isthmus of Panama on foot. Some of them, including the *Batchelor's Delight*, formed an uneasy alliance to attack a Spanish treasure convoy. In the ensuing fray, three French captains in the pirate flotilla, François Grognier, Pierre le Picard, and Raveneau de

Lussan, failed to support the badly damaged *Batchelor's Delight*, so the English decided to avoid the unreliable French corsairs in the future.

Following this incident, hastily armed Spanish government ships gave chase, so the English aboard the *Batchelor's Delight* sailed due west from Chile for several weeks, placing them far enough out in the vast Pacific to shake their pursuers. They spotted the long, high coast of an unknown land, which they called Davisland in honor of their new captain. Historians assume they were the first westerners ever to see the east coast of what we now know as New Zealand. When the French explorer Marion du Fresne and the famous British mariner James Cook visited New Zealand in the 1770s, many of their men were eaten by the native Maoris, so it was probably lucky that Davis, just as he had done at Easter Island, gave strict orders that no member of the crew should go ashore.

If they had gone ashore, they might have seen giant moas—mostly nocturnal, wingless, flightless birds whose females stood up to sixteen feet tall and weighed six hundred pounds, the size of giraffes. Preying on the moas were Haast's eagles, whose wings spanned up to fourteen feet, more than two feet greater than the wingspread of any bird living today. Both species of giant birds became extinct not long after the visit by the *Batchelor's Delight*. Although Dampier and Wafer never mentioned either of these birds in their journals, it is possible that the ship's lookout may have seen them and simply assumed it was the aftereffects of drinking too much rum.

While running along the west coast of South America, Davis's ship sacked Guayaquil, Ecuador, and raided various other ports, including Leon and El Realejo in Nicaragua, Paita and Arica in Chile, and Sana in Peru. The impressive ruins of Sana, destroyed by a natural disaster thirty-five years later, are now a tourist attraction featuring reminders of the city's encounter with the pirates. On one occasion, when the men of the *Batchelor's Delight* captured a Spanish ship carrying a cargo of slaves from Africa, they set the prisoners free and welcomed several into their crew.

William Dampier eventually tired of life on the *Batchelor's Delight* and became navigator of Captain Charles Swan's *Cygnet*, another former Spanish merchant ship captured by English buccaneers. He then sailed west across the Pacific to complete his second voyage around the world.

In mid-1687, Captain Davis and the crew of the *Batchelor's Delight* came to the conclusion that they had experienced all the adventures they wanted and gained enough treasure to last them a lifetime. Their decision may have had something to do with the fact that King James II was about to be thrown out by Parliament and replaced by his daughter Mary and her husband, William of Orange of the Netherlands. Life in England would undoubtedly be better under William III and Mary than it had been under James. More to the immediate point, however, was the news that James had just signed a proclamation offering amnesty to pirates who registered with the English authorities. Therefore, the men of the *Batchelor's Delight* decided to give up the sea and sail back to England.

Being fully aware of their precarious position, however, the adventurers wisely took some precautions. They buried about one-third of their treasure at Chatham Bay on the north coast of Cocos Island, three hundred miles off the coast of Costa Rica, in case they were somehow deprived of the rest of their loot on the way home. It is said that the five-mile-long Cocos Island, now Isla del Coco National Park, is the site of no fewer than three treasures from separate pirate ships, but although treasure seekers have mounted many expeditions over the years, no one has ever found anything of value.

Several of the crew, who had lost their shares through gambling, asked to be put ashore on Juan Fernandez Island as the ship headed south past Chile. What became of them is not recorded, but they were probably rescued by a visiting ship within a short period of time.

The *Batchelor's Delight* rounded Cape Horn in dreadful weather in the autumn of 1687. When the ship safely reached the Atlantic, Dr. Wafer called a meeting of the entire crew in which he laid out their situation as he understood it. Although they had initially set sail as privateers with letters of marque from King Charles II, not only did England have a new (and soon to be newer) monarch, but they also had attacked towns and vessels that did not fall within their job description. They were, in fact, pirates and would all have to be very careful. They could not expect a heroes' welcome after so much time and so many black deeds. Wafer went on to explain that if they all appeared in England at the same time with their mountain of booty, they would inevitably be recognized as pirates and hanged in spite of the letters of marque—which, to complicate matters further, had been issued for the *Revenge* under Captain Cooke, not for the *Batchelor's Delight* under the command of Captain Davis.

Wafer proposed that the crew draw lots. Those with the three shortest straws would disembark in Jamaica with their share of the loot, those with the next three shortest would land in the Bahamas, the next three in South Carolina, and so forth. The remaining men would sell the *Batchelor's Delight* in Philadelphia and take passage to other colonies on coastal ferries. After remaining in the colonies for two or three years, they could drift back to England if they wanted to. All agreed. Captain Davis accepted a royal pardon for the entire crew from the governor at Port Royal, Jamaica. He let it be known that the treasure to be divided among the crew came to more than 50,000 Spanish dollars, plus countless jewels and silver and gold plate.

In due course, their trusty ship was sold in Philadelphia, apparently to one or more of the old crew members, and she later surfaced on the other side of the world, where she was still plying the pirate's trade.

After the sale of the *Batchelor's Delight*, Lionel Wafer and Edward Davis, along with seaman John Hingson and a former Spanish slave named Peter Cloise, drew lots sending them to Virginia. They sailed down the Chesapeake Bay from Philadelphia on a local ferry and dropped off three other crewmen in Sussex County in what later became Delaware. This group started a plantation they named Bachelor's Delight, located where the village of Laurel now stands. In Maryland, a crewman named Berry and presumably two colleagues were the next to be dropped off. Here Berry obtained land in Charles County, also naming it Batchelor's Delight. Wafer, Davis, Hingson, and Cloise dutifully registered as ex-pirates and loyal British subjects with Commander Thomas Allen of HMS *Quaker*. Wafer and Davis even managed to deposit their loot in a Virginia bank. Lionel Wafer said he intended to settle in Norfolk, Virginia, so he, Davis, and Hingson set off in a launch for the coastline with the remaining portion of their booty.

When they reached Jamestown, the three were immediately arrested under suspicion of piracy on an order signed by Captain Simon Rowe of HMS *Dumbarton*. Rowe said he was acting under orders of Admiral Sir Robert Holmes, whose vigorous antipirate campaign stepped on the toes of many colonial officials. Captain Davis apparently had been recognized, and it seems the royal pardon the men had received in Jamaica was not acceptable to Virginia's powers that be.

The judge at Jamestown was nervous. He was aware that the *Batch-elor's Delight* had deposited crewmen along the Eastern Seaboard from Philadelphia all the way down to Jamaica. He was terrified that if he found Davis, Wafer, and Hingson guilty, other loyal pirates might sail up the James River and destroy Jamestown. Hoping to avoid the entire mess, he conveniently ignored the English constitution's guarantee of a speedy trial and left the men to languish in jail for nearly three years.

Eventually, their lawyer, a man named Perry, assisted by Virginia's new governor, Francis Nicholson, got them released on the newly instituted writ of habeas corpus. Perry was able to strike a deal with the judge that they would be sent to London for trial, despite a clause in the English Bill of Rights of 1689 that guaranteed trial in the court-house closest to the arrest.

Captain Rowe and Admiral Holmes, the men who had ordered Davis, Wafer, and Hingson's arrest, desperately tried to gain posses-sion of the loot but managed to confiscate only a portion of it. Mean-while, the three pirates' former companion and freed slave, Peter Cloise, who was the principal witness against them, had died. The three men sailed without escort or restraint to London aboard the merchant ship *Effingham* in late 1690, their good behavior ensured by their loot being loaded aboard a different ship. Once in London, the men were freed on bail but had to wait more than eighteen months for their trial in 1692.

During the trial, the judge told the three men that he was con-vinced in his heart that they really were pirates but felt the prosecution had not presented its case properly. So he offered them a plea bargain: if they were to donate a large portion of their loot to the reigning monarchs, King William III and Queen Mary II, who would use it for some charitable purpose, the court would exonerate them.

This strange-sounding offer was not unusual, since the Crown had recently offered to pardon all English pirates who fulfilled certain con-ditions. The three men readily complied and their monarchs issued this order: "It is this day ordered in council that the money, plate, jew-els and other goods belonging to said petitioners and seized by Cap-tain Rowe, now lying in their Majesties' warehouse or wherever, the same may be forthwith restored to the petitioners."

The king and queen observed that the alleged pirates had been arrested in Virginia, and since a delegation from Virginia had recently petitioned the Crown for financial assistance to establish a college there, William and Mary decided that their share of the pirate money should help found the college. The college was duly established in 1693, with the former pirate loot (the college's portion came to about 1,000 pounds sterling, with a purchasing power in today's monetary equivalent of over $1 million) supplemented by some Virginia rents collected by the Crown.

The college's single building was constructed of brick, supposedly based on designs donated by Sir Christopher Wren, at the village of Middle Plantation, about six miles from Jamestown. Named the College of William & Mary after its royal benefactors, it was only the second permanent college established in English America. Six years later, the village of Middle Plantation was greatly enlarged to make it the new capital of Virginia, and the colonists renamed it Williamsburg after King William III. Governor Nicholson, an amateur architect, devised the street plan and designed the capitol. Sadly, no building at the college has ever been named in tribute to its real benefactors, Davis, Wafer, and Hingson, nor has any memorial ever been made at the College of William & Mary to the *Batchelor's Delight*.

Lionel Wafer, who was now immune from further prosecution, wrote a book about his exploits and his observations on the Cuna Indians. Entitled *A New Voyage & Description of the Isthmus of America*, it was published in 1695. The rare-book section of the College of William & Mary's Earl Gregg Swem Library contains a first-edition copy, which anthropologists and naturalists still find useful. When Wafer began work on a second book in 1696, he enlisted the help of his old friend William Dampier, who had left his job as navigator on the pirate ship *Cygnet* in 1691. Together they incorporated their adventures on the *Batchelor's Delight* into a book entitled *A New Voyage Round the World*, published in 1697 and also included in the College of William & Mary library.

Captain Edward Davis, the *Batchelor's Delight*'s second captain, returned to Jamaica shortly after Port Royal was destroyed by a devastating earthquake in 1692. Davis returned to piracy, but Jamaica was no longer the pirate haven it had once been, so he sailed into the Indian Ocean. Here he encountered former shipmate James Kelley, who had rediscovered the venerable old *Batchelor's Delight* at St. Mary's Island near Madagascar and had subsequently been elected her new captain.

The *Batchelor's Delight* spent many years based at Saint Mary's and Fort Dauphin (now called Faradofay and Taolagnaro, respectively), at the southeast corner of Madagascar, and cruised among the Comoros Islands, the Seychelles, Reunion, and Mauritius before being taken by Muslim pirates near present-day Mumbai, India. The crew was tortured and murdered, and the *Batchelor's Delight* disappeared from history.

No one knows what became of the fortune in gold, silver, and gems that the crew of *Batchelor's Delight* buried near Chatham Bay shortly before they disbanded. There is no record of any crewman ever returning to claim it, and as no treasure has ever been located on the island, it may well still be buried there to this day.

William Kidd and the *Adventure Galley*

By April 1699, important orders from the lords justice of England had arrived in Virginia. These orders directed the governor and council to be on the lookout for a buccaneer named William Kidd, who was commanding the ship *Adventure Galley*.

Countless books have been written about the life and exploits of the infamous Captain Kidd, and to go into exhaustive detail about his adventures and misadventures is beyond the scope of this small book. But it is necessary to look at the highlights of his career as a pirate and privateer to understand his connection with the Virginia coast.

Kidd was born in Scotland around 1645. His father died when he was five years old, and the Kidd family immigrated to New York Colony. Kidd grew up in New York and apparently spent at least some time as a seaman's apprentice before beginning his own seafaring exploits.

The earliest surviving historical records for Kidd date from 1689, when he was about forty-four years old and a member of a pirate crew sailing in the Caribbean. Kidd and other members of the crew had mutinied, ousted the captain of the ship, and sailed to the English colony of Nevis. There they renamed their confiscated ship the *Blessed William*.

Either by popular election among the crew or by appointment of Christopher Codrington, governor of the island of Nevis, Kidd was made captain of the *Blessed William*. This ship became part of a small

43

fleet assembled by Codrington to defend Nevis from the French, with whom the English were at war. However Kidd acquired his captaincy, he must have been an experienced leader and sailor by that time. As the governor had no money to pay the sailors for their defensive services, he told them they could take their pay from the French. Thus the *Blessed William* became a privateering ship with letters of marque to attack any French ship or settlement. In due course, Kidd and his men attacked the French island of Mariegalante, destroyed and pillaged its only town, and quickly amassed a fortune in excess of 2,000 pounds sterling.

Shortly after their conquest of Mariegalante, Kidd agreed to ally the *Blessed William* with the British Royal Navy in a massed battle against French warships. Many members of Kidd's crew considered this a dangerous waste of time, since ships of war carried no treasure. The disagreement turned ugly and the men turned against their captain. Kidd tried to explain that they were working for the British and were therefore obligated to aid the Royal Navy, but his words fell on deaf ears. When Kidd rowed ashore while his ship was anchored at Nevis, his crew stole the *Blessed William* along with the looted French fortune stashed in its hold.

Governor Codrington courteously provided Kidd with another ship and gave him leave to hunt down the mutineers. Kidd sailed from Nevis, intending to do just that, but once at sea he lost their trail and eventually sailed to his hometown, New York City. Despite being a British colony, New York was, at the time, in open revolt against the British. Loyal to the Crown, Kidd offered to carry guns and ammunition for the British. In reward for his loyalty, the provincial assembly gave him 150 pounds sterling and lavish praises.

During his time in New York, Kidd met Sarah Bradley Cox Oort. Her second husband, John Oort, was a wealthy gentleman who owned several docks, as well as most of what is now Wall Street. Shortly after Kidd met Mrs. Oort, her husband died mysteriously, and although no one has ever discovered the truth behind John Oort's death, some historians believe Kidd killed him, or at least speeded his passage into the next world—perhaps with the aid of Sarah. Suspiciously, only two days after Oort's sudden death, Kidd and the recently widowed Sarah applied for a marriage license.

Now twice widowed and thrice married, Sarah Kidd inherited her former husband's fortune. Although William Kidd apparently loved his wife and the two daughters she brought to the marriage, according to the law of the day, he gained control over all of his wife's money and property. At a single stroke, Kidd became a very rich man with land and shipping docks, a position among New York's wealthy elite, and thanks to the generosity of Governor Codrington, a ship called the *Antigua*. Although Kidd easily could have retired from the sea, he remained restless.

Looking for a productive use of his time, by the spring of 1695 Kidd came up with a scheme. He decided to address the constant problem of marauding pirates who were disrupting British shipping by sailing to pirate-infested waters and randomly taking pirates into custody. He would then "recover" the booty the captured pirates had plundered from other ships and divide it among several investors. With this slightly shady, convoluted plan in mind, he enlisted the support of Richard Coote, who was the Earl of Bellomont and also the governor general of New York Colony, and Robert Livingston, an enterprising young Scot who had settled in New York City. Endorsed by the former and accompanied by the latter, Kidd visited London, where he formed a consortium to furnish the funds necessary to carry out his design.

King William III enthusiastically supported Kidd's plan, partly because the pirates were cutting off England's shipping and partly because he would receive a cut of the profits. The key, Kidd and Livingston knew, was to leave English ships untouched but hunt those of other countries—particularly Portugal, France, and Spain. Under this scheme, they could enjoy a life of piracy and privateering while remaining protected by the official sponsorship of the king of England. Besides Kidd, Livingston, and Coote, the venture included the Duke of Shrewsbury, the Earls of Romney and Oxford, Sir Edmund Harrison, Lord Chancellor John Somers, and other notables. As foster father of the expedition, King William was to receive one-tenth of any proceeds.

The king granted Kidd two letters of marque. The first entitled Kidd to apprehend "pirates, free-booters, and sea-rovers, being our subjects or of other nations associated with them," and to take pirates of any nationality—some of whom, notably Thomas Tew, were specifically named—and authorized him to seize them and their vessels wherever he found them. If they resisted, Kidd was authorized to use all necessary force in subduing them. The second letter of marque granted permission to take any ships belonging to France or its allies.

Kidd's only limitation was that he was not allowed to attack legitimate English ships or those of England's allies.

By August 1696, the eight contributing partners purchased a ship, the *Adventure Galley*, for 6,000 pounds sterling. The noble lords, who were both investors and among the most powerful men in England, paid four-fifths of the cost of the ship and its venture.

At over 284 tons, the *Adventure Galley*, was well suited to the task of catching pirates; she carried thirty-two cannons, and although it was a rarity for warships of the time, she had forty-six sweeps (oars), which allowed the crew to row the ship when necessary. Under full sail, she could travel at a respectable fourteen knots; under oar, without wind, she could make three knots. The oars were a key advantage, as they would enable the *Adventure Galley* to maneuver in battle when the winds had calmed and other ships were forced to sit immobile.

As the entire enterprise was speculative, the crew would sail without wages, their only pay being their share in any booty and prize money. Kidd and Livingston alone underwrote the expedition, agreeing to pay all expenses not met by its results. Should the ships take 100,000 pounds sterling or more in booty, Captain Kidd was to have the *Adventure Galley* given to him as a bonus. The success of the expedition therefore depended on seizing either French ships or pirates. Kidd's agreement with the backers stipulated that he had one year to hunt down prizes. If he failed to return with the promised booty by March 25, 1697, Captain Kidd would owe them 20,000 pounds sterling.

In April 1696, the *Adventure Galley* departed from England with a crew of about 140 men. As they sailed down the Thames, Kidd unaccountably failed to salute a Royal Navy vessel at Greenwich, as custom dictated. The navy ship then fired a shot to make him show respect, and in a shocking display of impudence, Kidd's crew reportedly responded by turning around and slapping their exposed backsides at the passing ship. This did not herald an auspicious beginning to the voyage.

The navy vessel retaliated by stopping the *Adventure Galley* and pressing many of her crewmen into service. Thus short-handed, Kidd sailed for New York, but he still managed to capture a small French merchant vessel en route. To make up for his lack of men, Kidd picked up replacement crew members in New York, the vast majority of whom were known to be hardened criminals, some undoubtedly former pirates. Governor Benjamin Fletcher of New York wrote to the

Board of Trade about Kidd's crew: "Many flocked to him from all parts, men desperate of fortunes and necessities, in expectation of getting vast treasure. It is generally believed here that if he misses the design named in his commission, he will not be able to govern such a villainous herd."

On September 10, 1696, the men signed eighteen articles of agreement under which they would sail. The contract "between Capt. William Kidd Commander of the good ship *Adventure Galley* on the one part and John Walker Quarter Master to the said ships company on the other part," included the following stipulations:

- That if any man shall lose an Eye, Legg or Arme or the use thereof . . . [he] shall receive . . . six hundred pieces of eight, or six able Slaves.
- The man who shall first see a Sail. If she be a Prize shall receive one hundred pieces of eight.
- That whosoever shall disobey Command shall lose his share or receive such Corporal punishment as the Capt. and Major part of the Company shall deem fit.
- That man is proved a Coward in time of Engagement shall lose his share.
- That man that shall be drunk in time of Engagement before the prisoners then taken be secured, shall lose his share.
- That man that shall breed a Mutiny Riot on Board the ship or Prize taken shall lose his share and receive such Corporal punishment as the Capt. and major part of the Company shall deem fit.
- That if any man shall defraud the Capt. or Company of any Treasure, as Money, Goods, Ware, Merchandizes or any other thing whatsoever to the value of one piece of eight . . . [he] shall lose his Share and be put on shore upon the first inhabited Island or other place that the said ship shall touch at.
- That what money or Treasure shall be taken by the said ship and Company shall be put on board the Man of War and there be shared immediately, and all Wares and Merchandizes when legally condemned to be legally divided amongst the ships Company according to Articles.

Although Kidd and his men sailed as privateers, these articles of agreement were more akin to those signed by pirate corporations than by sailors operating under letters of marque. Perhaps owing to the mutiny and theft of his ship and cargo earlier in his career, Kidd must have thought these articles a necessity to ensure that every man knew his place.

And so it was that in September 1696, Kidd weighed anchor and set course for the Cape of Good Hope at the southern tip of Africa. Although the wind and tides were with him, good fortune was not. Within a few weeks, a third of his crew were dead or dying as a result of a virulent outbreak of cholera, the newly built *Adventure Galley* was leaking, and worst of all, Kidd had failed to find any of the prizes he had expected to encounter off Madagascar. Growing desperate, he sailed the *Adventure Galley* northward to the Strait of Bab-el-Mandeb at the southern entrance of the Red Sea, a notorious pirate haunt. Again he failed to find any pirates. According to Edward Barlow, a captain employed by the British East India Company, Kidd attacked a Mughal convoy being escorted by an East Indian and was beaten off. If we are to believe this report, it marks Kidd's first foray into piracy while he was under the Crown's patronage.

As it became increasingly obvious that Kidd's ambitious enterprise was failing, he became more and more desperate to find a way of covering the costs of the expedition. The frustration must have taken a heavy toll on him, because on October 30, 1697, Kidd inadvertently killed one of his own crewmen. When a Dutch ship sailed into sight, Kidd's chief gunner, William Moore, urged Kidd to attack. But attacking a ship of England's ally would have been an act of piracy certain to anger England's Dutch-born King William III. Kidd refused, and a heated argument ensued. Infuriated, Kidd snatched up an bucket bound with iron hoops and struck Moore, who fell to the deck with a fractured skull and died the following day.

Although seventeenth-century admiralty law afforded captains great latitude in the degree of violence they used to govern unruly crewmen, outright murder was not permitted. But Kidd seemed unconcerned, later explaining to his surgeon that he had "good friends in England" that would get him off the hook. Some of the crew deserted when the *Adventure Galley* next made port, and those who stayed behind voiced constant discontent and made frequent open threats of mutiny.

Despite the endless litany of problems, on January 30, 1698, Kidd took his greatest prize, the Armenian-owned *Quedagh Merchant*, which was loaded with an incredible variety of merchandise from India, including satins, silks, and muslins along with gold and silver. It was a rich bounty and a tremendous prize. Unfortunately, the captain of the *Quedagh Merchant* was a less-than-patriotic Englishman named Wright, who had purchased passes from the French East India Company promising him the protection of the French Crown. After realizing that the captain of the taken vessel was an Englishman, Kidd tried to persuade his crew to return the ship to its owners. They refused, however, claiming that their prey was perfectly legal, as Kidd was commissioned to take French ships, and an Armenian ship counted as French if it had French passes. In an attempt to maintain his all-too-tenuous control over his crew, Kidd relented and kept the prize.

When news of the *Quedagh Merchant*'s fate reached England, it confirmed Kidd's reputation as a pirate, and various naval commanders were ordered to "pursue and seize the said Kidd and his accomplices" for the "notorious piracies" they had committed. Kidd kept the *Quedagh Merchant*'s French passes, as well as the vessel herself. Although the passes were at best a dubious defense of his actions, British admiralty and vice admiralty courts, especially in North America, had often turned a blind eye at privateers' trespasses into piracy, and Kidd may have been hoping that the passes would provide legal justification that would allow him to keep the *Quedagh Merchant* and her cargo. Renaming the seized merchantman the *Adventure Prize*, he set sail for Madagascar.

Kidd finally reached Madagascar on April 1, 1698, and here he encountered the first actual pirate vessel of his voyage, the *Mocha Frigate*, captained by Robert Culliford—the same man who had stolen Kidd's ship, the *Blessed William*, years earlier. Two contradictory accounts exist of how Kidd reacted to his encounter with Culliford.

According to one account, Kidd made peaceful overtures to Culliford: he "drank their Captain's health," swearing that "he was in every respect their Brother," and gave Culliford "a Present of an Anchor and some Guns." This account appears to be based on the testimony of two of Kidd's crewmen at his trial. The other version contends that Kidd was unaware that Culliford had only about twenty crewmen and believed that he was undermanned and ill equipped to take the *Mocha Frigate* until his two prize ships and crews arrived, so he decided not to molest Culliford until reinforcements came. After the *Adventure Prize* and *Rouparelle* appeared, Kidd ordered his crew to attack Culliford's *Mocha Frigate*. But his crew, despite their previous eagerness to seize any available prize, refused to attack Culliford and threatened to shoot Kidd. Whichever version of the encounter is true, two things are certain: Kidd had failed to capture the *Mocha Frigate*—the only genuine pirate vessel he encountered in his expedition to hunt and capture pirates—and his crew was teetering on the brink of mutiny.

Kidd now resolved to return with his booty and prizes to New York, disband the current crew, divide the spoils, and refit the ships. En route to New York, however, Kidd learned that he had been declared a pirate and several English men-of-war were searching for him to claim the bounty on his head. Realizing that the *Adventure Prize* was a marked vessel, he disposed of it in the Caribbean and continued toward New York aboard a small sloop. He stopped at several places along the Virginia coastline and secreted treasure away in various hiding places, hoping to use his knowledge of its location as a bargaining chip in the inevitable fight to clear his name and save his skin.

Back in England, the lords justice had, in compliance with the forceful persuasion of the immensely powerful East India Company, directed all colonial governors to apprehend and secure Kidd and his associates in order that they might be "prosecuted to ye utmost rigor of law." If Kidd or any of his crew were apprehended in Virginia or Maryland, they were to be held until the king issued further commands.

Governor Nicholson dutifully directed all of the colony's militia commanders, sheriffs, customs agents, and naval officers to be on the alert and apprehend the pirates should they enter Old Dominion waters or make landfall anywhere along the coastline. A few days later, formal notices and proclamations were posted throughout Maryland and Virginia authorizing the capture of the pirates by any loyal colonial citizens.

After numerous false reports, false alarms, and a few false arrests, fears of pirate incursion only escalated once word arrived from the sheriff of Accomack County that Kidd had arrived on the coast. The collector of customs for the Eastern Shore, it seems, had told the sheriff that two ex-pirates named Stretcher and Lewis had informed him of Kidd's arrival on the Delaware. The two had been aboard Kidd's ship, which, they reported, boasted forty-two guns and was accompanied by an eighteen-gun sloop. At least 130 pirates were aboard the two vessels, they said, although a handful of them had taken their leave, some en route to Philadelphia, and others shipping aboard a sloop belonging to Andrew Gravenrod and bound for Maryland. The pirates were heavily laden with plunder and booty, with their ships carrying "30 Tunns of Gold and Silver aboard," and the pair claimed that each of their company had a share equivalent to 4,000 pounds sterling. Kidd apparently felt secure on the waters of the Chesapeake, as he reportedly sent word to his wife in New York to join him, but she never arrived.

In Virginia governor Nicholson's view, the coastline lay under imminent threat and peril. One of the world's most-wanted criminals lay within striking distance. Both Maryland and Virginia worried about reports that as many as sixty deserters, and more than a few pirates who had been captured and subsequently escaped jail, were intending to swarm into the Tidewater region of the Chesapeake Bay. The threat posed by the infamous Captain Kidd and the sixty deserters from his crew had already become a veritable nightmare for Robert Quary of the Vice Admiralty Court of Pennsylvania. With the aid of Governor Jeremiah Basse of New Jersey, he was able to capture four of the pirates at Cape May and wrote:

> And might have with Ease secured all the rest of them, and the ship too, had not this Government given me the Least aide or assistance, but they [did] not, or soe much as Issue out a Proclamation. But on the Contrary the People of the Government have Entertain'd the Pyrates, Conveyed them from place to place, Furnish'd them with Provisions and Liquors given them Inteli'gence and sheltered them from Justice, and now the greatest part of them are conveyed away in Boats to Road Island [*sic*]. All the person[s] That I have affronted and call'd Enemies to the Country for Disturbing and hindring honest men (as They are pleased to call the Pyrates) from bringing their money and Settling amongst them.

Judging from Quary's words, it would seem that the deserter pirates were able to purchase cooperation from local officials and citizens alike. Certainly, the individual shares of loot amounting to 4,000 pounds sterling per man would have financed a lot of bribes and purchased a tremendous welcome and goodwill.

In complete desperation, Quary dispatched an express to Governor Nicholson begging him to immediately send a man-of-war to patrol the Delaware River. Nicholson responded by sending the *Essex Prize* "to look About for Sixty Pyrates (which belonged to one Captain Kidd) who came from Madagascar." But by the time the *Essex Prize* got there, the Delaware was empty. The pirates were gone.

Unbeknownst to Governor Nicholson, Kidd had set sail for Boston, stopping briefly en route at Gardiners Island off the coast of New York Colony. Although Kidd's friend and co-investor, colonial Governor Coote, the Earl of Bellomont, was in Boston, he was well aware of the accusations against Kidd and was justifiably afraid of being implicated in his associate's acts of piracy. Bellomont reasoned that his best chance of saving his own neck was to send Kidd to England in chains. On July 1, 1699, Kidd's sloop arrived in Boston, but Kidd did not go to the governor's house until the evening of July 3. The next day, he gave Bellomont a detailed narrative of the voyage and the names of his crew and the mutineers. Several days later, Bellomont issued an arrest warrant, and Kidd was taken to jail and all his possessions were seized. The governor sent a letter informing the Board of Trade in England that he had captured the infamous William Kidd.

Kidd attempted to escape from jail and was moved to Stone Prison, where he was put in irons and denied all visitors. Kidd's wife, Sarah, petitioned for the return of belongings she had brought to her husband's ship, which had been confiscated along with his other holdings. Although she had no communication with Kidd, Sarah seems to have remained steadfastly loyal to him while he spent his days in an unheated cell, waiting for a chance to clear his name. On February 16, 1700, he was taken aboard HMS *Advice*, on which he endured the long crossing to London while chained to the wall of a cabin. Sarah never got to say good-bye.

Kidd's return to England threatened to cause a political scandal because of his links to King William and the four powerful Whig politicians who had backed his voyage. In a deposition taken during a seven-hour grilling before the Lords of the Admiralty, Kidd said that he "was employed for the seizing of pirates . . . ; only as to his own committing piracy he would excuse himself that his seamen forced him to what was done." The Tories accused the Whigs of hiring a pirate to steal for them. Robert Harley, Speaker of the House of Commons, said,

"Captain Kidd was commander under the Great Seal of England to go against pirates at Madagascar. . . . That several great men were to have shares with him, amongst whom the pirates' goods were to be divided, whereas by law, they should [have been] returned to the owners. . . . It is said the Great Seal [Somers] and others are concerned in it." The true reasons for his arrest and imprisonment had become clear: Kidd was a pawn in the political maneuverings of the British Parliament, and like all pawns, he was entirely expendable. Kidd was imprisoned in Newgate Prison and held in solitary confinement. He could write only to the Admiralty, and no one was permitted to talk with him.

While imprisoned for piracy and murder, Kidd told authorities that a small portion of his fabulous treasure was hidden on Gardiners Island, New York, where a friend was safeguarding it. In fact, Kidd had left it in the care of John Gardiner, who owned the island. Gardiner cooperated with British authorities in retrieving the loot. Following Kidd's instructions, gold and other treasure worth in excess of 10,000 pounds sterling was dug up on Gardiners Island and sent to England to pay off his investment backers in the hope of ensuring their loyalty. This seems to have had the opposite effect from what Kidd intended. Some of the backers refused to accept payment lest it implicate them as culpable in Kidd's actions. Those who did receive payment simply saw it as just return on their investment and wanted nothing more to do with the matter. In total, 1,111 ounces of gold, 2,353 ounces of silver, one pound of assorted gemstones, fifty-seven bags of sugar, and forty-one bales of cloth were shipped to the English Treasury. Precisely how much of Kidd's Gardiners Island fortune actually made its way back to England is unknown, but amazingly, Gardiners Island is still privately owned by the Gardiner family, four hundred years after Kidd's death.

Whether or not this was a desperate political maneuver, Kidd also indicated that further treasures were hidden in Virginia, New Jersey, and elsewhere, and that they could be retrieved if only someone would step forward to intercede on his behalf. But as with the Gardiners Island treasure, no one wanted to ally himself with Kidd even for the sake of a vast fortune, so knowledge of the exact location of the rest of Kidd's treasure remained his and his alone.

On March 27, 1701, one day short of a year after entering Newgate Prison, Kidd became history's only accused pirate to testify before

Britain's House of Commons. The four hundred members of Parliament shouted questions, and although no precise transcript exists, we know that Kidd denied being a pirate and refused to implicate his backers in the supposed scandal in the hope that his show of loyalty to his investors would persuade them to intercede on his behalf. But like most political loyalties, it was naïve and wholly misplaced.

William Kidd's trial began two weeks later, on May 8, and ended the following day. Five prosecutors tried him, and nine others—six loyal members of his crew and three mutineers—testified. Kidd refused to plead until he had the French passes taken from the *Quedagh Merchant*, but eventually he pleaded not guilty. For two years, Kidd had been accused of being a pirate, but now the primary charge against him was not for piracy, but for the murder of gunner William Moore. The jury brought a unanimous guilty verdict.

Kidd was then tried again, this time for piracy. Doctor Newton, the prosecutor, said Kidd had "committed many great piracies and robberies, taking the ships and goods of the Indians and others . . . and torturing cruelly their persons to discover if anything had escaped his hands; burning their houses, and killing after a barbarous manner the Natives on shore; equally cruel, dreaded and hated both on land and at sea. These criminal attempts and actions have rendered his name . . . too well known [and] he is now looked upon as an Arch Pirate and Common Enemy of Mankind."

After this withering—and creatively enhanced—opening statement, Newton called his witnesses. Doctor Bradinham testified that Kidd had fired on English ships, kidnapped an English captain, tortured passengers, executed a native who had been tied to a tree, and burned a village. He denied any knowledge of the French passes, but Kidd's former crewman, Joseph Palmer, confirmed that Kidd had taken them. This second jury found Kidd guilty in thirty minutes.

Now that Kidd had twice been found guilty of capital crimes, his prosecutors reportedly turned to him and inquired, "Thou hast been indicted for several Piracies and Robberies, and Murder, and hereupon hast been convicted. What hast thou to say for thyself, why shouldest thou not die according to law?" Kidd replied, "I have nothing to say, but that I have been sworn against by perjured and wicked People." The sentence, as expected, was death by hanging. Kidd's only comment on hearing his fate was "My Lord, it is a very hard sentence. For my part, I am the innocentest person of them all, only I have been sworn against by perjured persons." During his trial, a member of Parliament had said of Kidd, "I thought him only a knave. I now know him to be a fool as well."

Kidd's execution was set for late afternoon on Friday, May 23. Having drunk a considerable amount of rum before and during the three-mile procession to Execution Dock, he slurred his words while giving his last speech, in which he blamed his mutinous crew for his troubles and named his New York patrons, Robert Livingston and the colony's governor general, the Earl of Bellomont, as villains. When he finished, the hangman yanked the blocks holding up the platform, and Kidd and three others dropped. Kidd's rope broke and he fell to the ground, but the reprieve was short-lived. The executioner immediately picked him up, affixed another rope, and promptly hanged him again. His corpse was hung in an iron gibbet at Tilbury Point to serve as a deterrent—"as a greater Terrour to all Persons from Committing ye like Crimes for the time to come."

Thus conclude the adventures and misadventures of the infamous, and rather ineffective, pirate known as Captain William Kidd. But Kidd's undignified end marked the beginning of his legend. For four centuries, people have wondered what became of the buried treasures he claimed to have secreted away along the Virginia coast. The truth about Kidd's supposed Virginia treasure—both its size and its whereabouts—seems to have gone to the grave (or the gibbet) with Captain Kidd.

But the death of Captain Kidd unfortunately did not mark the beginning of peaceful and calm waters on the Chesapeake Bay. The worst pirate invasion and infestation in American maritime history had just begun.

John James and the *Providence Galley*

J ohn James was ugly and mean. By all accounts, James was a far cry from the dashing hero rogues that populate ships and terrorize the waves in fictional pirate stories. He was ugly, aggressive, and severely disfigured by smallpox. Of average height, James was square shouldered, bony jointed, with a blemish in his left eye that gave him a squinty, surly, sinister aspect, and he spoke with a broad, thick Welsh accent. He was bold and egotistical, and he is known to have made comparisons between himself and the infamous and legendary Captain William Kidd.

In 1697, James was a crew member on the *Providence Frigate*, a pirate ship captained by a ruthless Dutch buccaneer named Hynd, who busied himself marauding across the Caribbean Sea from the Bay of Campeche to the Bahamas. For reasons that remain lost to history, at some point during his time on the *Providence Frigate*, James led the crew in a mutiny before taking command of the ship. He then marooned Captain Hynd, along with fifteen crewmen who remained loyal to their captain, on the Berry Islands, ten leagues leeward of New Providence in the Bahamas. He left them with only three pistols and a bottle of gunpowder to face their fate. This was typical in cases of marooning, not so much for defense against threat, but for the purposes of suicide should the marooning end in starvation or disease.

Along with command of the *Providence Frigate,* James also took control of a small flotilla of vessels that had fallen prey to Hynd. Captain James sailed his little armada to New Providence, where his new flagship was repaired, refitted, and resupplied. Four additional cannons were brought aboard, bringing the vessel's armament to a full twenty-six guns. But the ship needed further refitting and repairs, so Captain John James took several of the island's inhabitants hostage as leverage to get the others to work on the flagship and the captured prizes—which they did while his men enjoyed some debauched shore leave. After the prizes had been refitted and repaired and the flagship rearmed, James sold off the prizes, stowed the gold in the hold of his ship—now renamed the *Providence Galley*—and set off in search of new prizes.

The specific details of this cruise are unknown. However, we can assume that Captain James and the crew of the *Providence Galley* must have captured many prizes and succeeded in hunting down wealthy prey, because in July 1699, as they were approaching the coast of Virginia and the Chesapeake Bay, James boasted of having accumulated several million pounds sterling in gold, silver, and loot from captured vessels.

What drove James into the Chesapeake was not a quest for further wealth, but a desperate need for provisions, rigging, guns, and anchors. As the *Providence Galley* cruised off the Virginia coast in mid-July, her string of conquests continued. James's first victim in Virginia waters was a pink—a shallow-drafted ship with a narrow, overhanging stern—named the *Hope*, which had sailed from the James River on July 23 en route home to London. Although the *Hope* was not a particularly valuable prize, her capture was a remarkable stroke of good fortune for James, because it was carrying government documents of great interest to the pirates. Among these documents were six months' worth of record books belonging to the guard ship *Essex Prize*. These records contained strategic information describing the tragically weak status of Virginia's naval defenses. Such data suggested intriguing possibilities to Captain James. Interrogation of the crewmen of the *Hope* further substantiated the documents' information, and Captain James learned that at least two of the *Hope*'s crewmen had been aboard the *Essex Prize* earlier that very morning. Using techniques typical of men like John James, the unhappy crewmen were "persuaded" to reveal information about the guard ship's size, company, weaknesses, and even the temperamental nature of her captain, a man named Aldred. But most notably, James learned that the *Essex Prize* was the only guard ship defending the entirety of the Chesapeake Bay.

It did not take the pirates long to realize the potential offered by the Virginia Colony's nearly defenseless position, and they were eager to profit by it. Realizing that the *Providence Galley* was far superior to the *Essex Prize* in both artillery and manpower, they decided to capture the *Essex Prize* and plunder her of her sails, rigging, and other stores. Then they would proceed up the Chesapeake Bay, which would lie defenseless against attack, and Captain James would make easy prey of the valuable cargo ships making their way in and out of the bay.

On July 24, 1699, as HMS *Essex Prize* lay at anchor in four fathoms of water, five miles northwest of Cape Henry, a raging storm struck the Virginia Capes, driving merciless walls of wind and rain hard up the Chesapeake. At three o'clock the next morning, the already ferocious gale intensified further. Although the guard ship was secured firmly with three anchors, she buckled with every gale, gust, and surge of the roiling waters. She suffered serious storm damage and nearly capsized but managed to survive nature's fury. But unbeknownst to the men of the *Essex Prize*, an equally dangerous threat lay just beyond the horizon.

At four o'clock on the morning of July 26, as the first fingers of dawn lightened the eastern sky, the lookout on the *Essex Prize* spotted a strange ship entering Lynnhaven Bay. It appeared to be bearing down on the outward-bound *Maryland Merchant*, which had set sail on the early-morning tide with a cargo of tobacco bound for Bristol, England. His suspicions aroused, Captain Aldred ordered the crew of the *Essex Prize* to make sail. As they came within hailing distance, the crew on the strange ship hoisted the king's colors and a blood red flag to her maintop and fired guns both windward and leeward. But it was obvious that the cannons carried no balls, and the cannonade appeared to be a salute rather than an attack. As the guard ship maneuvered for position and revealed her identity, the pirates unleashed a withering broadside. Clearly this unidentified stranger was not one of the king's ships. Seeing the danger he was in, Captain Aldred gave the order to return fire.

Despite her initial bravado, the *Essex Prize*, with only sixteen guns and fewer than sixty men, was no match for the larger ship, which boasted twenty-six guns and 130 men. Fully aware that he was battling a pirate ship of great strength, Aldred decided the best course of action would be to draw the deep-drafted predator away from the *Maryland Merchant*, which lay three miles to the north, and into the shoals of the Virginia shore. When the *Essex Prize* "hove to," the pirate ship pursued her, with guns blazing.

Aldred recorded in his ship's log that in order to facilitate the escape of the *Maryland Merchant*, which was north of his position, "I kept a leading fight to ye Southward towards Cape Henry my master being well acquainted with ye shoals." Aldred obviously hoped to run the pirates aground, but the wily enemy was not about to be fooled and coasted just beyond the dangerous shallows. Finally, the *Providence Galley* tacked and stood off from the *Essex Prize*. Confronted with this standoff, Captain Aldred refused to abandon the game of harassing the intruder, but he wisely never committed his outgunned ship to full combat.

At this juncture, the *Maryland Merchant*, despite having a clear run to freedom, inexplicably bore down hard and fast on the pirate ship, "being to windward and sailing very well." Before the merchantman could get to the leeward of the intruder, the *Providence Galley* fired a single shot at her, striking her mainmast. The pirates ranged alongside the wounded vessel and commanded her master and his company to come aboard in their ship's launch. The pirates took the men from the boat and cut it loose, leaving the merchant vessel unmanned and at anchor. They then resumed their pursuit of the *Essex Prize*.

As Aldred had recently sent his longboat ashore with seven men, his onboard complement was severely weakened. The enemy had superior firepower, manpower, size, and speed. Seeing his position as both untenable and desperate, Aldred later wrote, "Ye pirate ship, being very clean, wronged me much." Captain Aldred was in every way outmatched, and it was becoming increasingly clear that the pirates intended to capture and board the *Essex Prize*. If "he had done so, he would have overpowered me with men," recorded Aldred.

The game of cat and mouse continued for long hours, with the *Essex Prize* attempting to draw the *Providence Galley* into the sandy shoals, but to no avail. Left with few viable options Aldred decided to make a run for it. He wrote in his log that he "thought it more service to make sail into ye shore to acquaint ye Governor thereof, to prevent his [the pirates'] doing any further damage and to make a strong defense against him." The *Maryland Merchant* was left to her fate at the hands of the pirates.

Once ashore, Aldred immediately sent a note to Governor Nicholson, outlining the narrative of the battle, such as it had been, and his reasons for abandoning the engagement. In defense of his actions, Aldred said he had left the battle to make the pirates' presence known in order to prevent other ships from sailing into the buccaneers' clutches and also to secure as many landsmen as possible, with which he "may deal with him [the pirates] & may keep him from doing any more damage."

The voracious pirates meanwhile had returned their attention to the *Maryland Merchant*. Captain Burgess, when finally confronted by the squinty, pockmarked buccaneer and his crew, was thoroughly intimidated. Amazingly, he was also impressed by the unexpectedly courteous demeanor of his captor. Having captured the merchant ship with a single shot and successfully chased off the only guard ship in the Chesapeake Bay, the pirates were feeling confident, boastful, and inclined to show off for their captives. They bragged about their conquests in the Caribbean and told tales of the immense fortune in the ship's hold—a treasure in gold and silver that they claimed to be worth more than three million pounds sterling. It was quickly apparent that the *Maryland Merchant* had little to offer the pirates in the way of booty. Captain Burgess later reported, "They thought it not worth their while to take a gentleman's plate and money, value nigh one hundred pounds, that was on board." Instead, they proceeded to strip the merchant vessel of her mainsail, topsail, spritsail, cables, and a hundred pounds of dry goods. They then pressed eight of the unlucky crewmen into service aboard the *Providence Galley*. As the pirates finished plundering the merchant vessel, Captain James asked his captive whom he thought the *Essex Prize* had been searching for. "Captain Kidd," replied Burgess somewhat timidly.

"I am Kidd," lied James. And Burgess believed him.

The pirates released the *Maryland Merchant*, but she was in such disabled condition, with almost all of her sails looted, that she was eventually driven helplessly aground to founder on the shoals of Willoughby Point.

When the sloop *Roanoke Merchant*, belonging to Colonel Robert Quary, sailed through the Virginia Capes on July 27, 1699, on the last leg of her journey from Barbados to Annapolis, nothing seemed out of the ordinary. Her commander, Captain Nicholas Thomas Jones, saw nothing unusual about the large ship anchored in Lynnhaven Bay, "under ye King's Colours, with [the Union] Jack, Ancient, and pendant aboard." He took it to be one of His Majesty's men-of-war, probably the Virginia guard ship *Essex Prize*, and thus took no evasive measures to avoid passing close by her.

Suddenly Captain Jones heard two cannons roar and a shout ordering him to heave to and come aboard the waiting ship. With little alternative, he obliged. Once aboard, he was greeted by Captain John James, who informed him with a smirk that had the *Roanoke Merchant* failed to follow his order to halt, she most assuredly would have been sunk. A quick glance at the unmilitary dress and nature of the crewmen aboard the warship confirmed Jones's doubt as to the true nature of the *Providence Galley*.

Under interrogation, Captain Jones readily divulged information about his cargo and destination, even handing over official clearance papers when the pirates demanded them. James then instructed Jones that he would be relieving the *Roanoke Merchant* of her provision stores of peas, pork, and tallow, "and what else he had occasion for." Relishing the stunned expression on the merchant commander's face, James then confirmed Captain Jones's suspicion: he had been taken by pirates.

Shortly afterward, as the pirates were escorting Jones to a holding area, a crewman named Lux approached him. Jones recognized the man as having sailed on the New York brig *Charles*, which had fallen prey to pirates sometime earlier. Lux calmed Jones, telling him that the pirate captain—whose identity he still did not know—would not harm him "otherwise than to take what he wanted or what he had a mind to." Which is precisely what John James and the crew of the *Providence Galley* proceeded to do. The plunder of the *Roanoke Merchant* was extensive, including

> sixteen barrel of porke, one Barrell of tallow, twenty nine Bushels of Beans, two Quoiles of Ropes, Six firelocks with all . . . Ammunicon, most of ye Carpenters tools, and diverse necessary Utensils for use, 1/2 Barrell of Tarr, Balls of Rope Yarn, long line and Reckle, several Cask of Water, and a quantity of

provision, by which about 30 or 40 barrels of Corn were damnifyed, fallen down to ye bottom of ye Sloop, likewise one barrel marked R.M. belonging to one Mr. Robert Mellam a passenger, one Bear skin & one Bever skin.

Later in the day, the pirate captain summoned Jones to his cabin. He was, he boasted, none other than Captain John James, a Welshman from Glamorganshire, and his ship was the *Alexander*, taken from "one Captain Watt [Rhett] of South Carolina about the Bay of Campeachy." After the brief, if largely inaccurate, introduction, he proceeded to make Captain Jones squirm and beg for mercy by loudly announcing his intention of impressing several of the *Roanoke Merchant*'s crewmen—perhaps even Jones himself—into his own company and then burning their ship. Jones begged him to forgo sinking the ship, an act that would bring absolute ruin to the ship's unfortunate owner, Colonel Quary. His begging had little effect, so Jones switched tactics to a show of strength, insisting that he was resolved not to join the pirates and would sooner burn with his ship.

Wearying of the game, James finally demanded that only two of the *Roanoke Merchant*'s crew be selected to join his company. Mate John Lukas and seaman William Steeward were compelled to sign the pirate articles, though they "appeared very unwilling, begging and earnestly entreating ye Captain for their liberty, but all in vain."

Around eight o'clock that evening, the quartermaster of the *Providence Galley* suggested it might be a prudent time to put to sea because some of the crew members were anxious to move on to more profitable pickings. Since the pirate articles required a consensus in such matters, the captain consulted the ship's complement to determine "what ye Company inclined to doe." They decided to explore other hunting grounds, but first they would have to figure out what to do with Captain Jones and the *Roanoke Merchant*.

As a final bit of pirate sport, James gave Jones the opportunity to publicly beg for the return of his sloop and men in front of both assembled crews. Finally, after repeated pleas, the buccaneers agreed to release Jones and his sloop, but they would retain the majority of his crew. The pirates had learned well from experience that as soon as they released Jones and his few remaining seamen, their former captives would relay all available intelligence to the royal authorities as soon as possible. In an effort to turn that inevitability to their advantage, James filled his prisoners' heads with frightening information. He told John Martin, the *Roanoke*'s master, of a second pirate ship that served as consort to the *Providence Galley*. She had eight guns and fifty men, he explained, and was lurking somewhere just off the Chesapeake Capes, awaiting word to bear down on the Virginia coast. The information about this phantom ship was designed to confuse and intimidate the authorities, which it did very well.

Meanwhile, Captain Jones, humiliated but relieved to have escaped unharmed, boarded his vessel with his remaining crewmen and made a hasty exit up the Chesapeake for Annapolis, before the pirates could change their fickle minds. Once in Maryland, he gave a full account of the affair directly to the governor, and then set about inventorying his losses.

By the time Captain Jones had reported the incident to the authorities, Captain John Aldred and the *Essex Prize* had spent several days anchored off Castle Point, near Hampton, while the captain licked his wounds and replaced his ship's shredded sails with new ones. While making repairs, Aldred dispatched the master of the *Essex Prize* to Lynnhaven Bay to gather intelligence concerning the pirates' whereabouts and strength. He soon found the grounded *Maryland Merchant* and received from Captain Burgess the grim details of the buccaneers' identity and strength, as well as a full account of their various captures. Upon his return to the *Essex Prize*, Aldred's ship's master reported the happy news that the pirates had departed, but he tempered it with the alarming intelligence that an alleged consort was waiting to pounce somewhere just beyond the Virginia Capes.

Aldred was undoubtedly dreading a second encounter with the well-armed and well-manned pirate ship, not to mention the threat of a second ship prowling nearby. He also likely was concerned that some people would question his lack of success in the previous encounter and might even consider him and his vessel unsuitable to patrol the waters of the Chesapeake. In his own defense, he quickly composed a "certificate" of the inadequacies of the guard ship and gave the letter to his ship's master with instructions to deliver it personally to Virginia governor Nicholson.

The governor and his council accepted the excuse, but Nicholson had grown impatient with Captain Aldred, whose apparent timidity in battle and unwillingness to seek information until after the pirates had long departed now fed a frustration that was quickly growing into animosity. Nicholson convened an urgent meeting of the council at Jamestown and angrily laid before it the letters from Aldred and related documents from Colonel William Wilson, militia commander of Elizabeth City County, concerning the pirate invasion. The council moved quickly; even though the immediate crisis had passed, they felt that more pirate landings in colonies to the north, as well as on the Virginia coast, were highly probable. The council sent notices to the governments of northerly colonies with descriptions of the pirates and their ships, as well as details of the crimes they had committed, in the hope that they might be captured and brought to trial.

It was painfully clear that more force and better protection were necessary if the pirates were to be stopped. Captain Aldred and the *Essex Prize* simply were not up to the task of safeguarding shipping along the entire Virginia coastline. The council therefore implored Nicholson to request that the king supply "a Ship of sufficient force to defend his Colony & Dominion agst pyrats, and yt there may be allowed to her a small Tender, which in case of Necessity, may serve as a fire Ship."

The government not only was distraught over the attacks on shipping, but also was equally concerned about the possibility of pirates landing on the Virginia coast. Pirates could blend in with the general population to escape punishment or conduct coastal raids to secure provisions before returning to sea. In answer to this threat, Nicholson issued a decree on August 9, 1699, directing the commanders of militia in the counties of Norfolk, Princess Anne, Accomac, Northampton, and Elizabeth City to appoint coast watchers, or lookouts, in each county to patrol the respective seacoasts until September 29. It was believed that after that date, the onset of autumn weather would significantly decrease the likelihood of pirate activity in Virginia waters until spring.

One lookout would pace the beach between Cape Henry and the Lynnhaven River. Another would patrol between Cape Henry and Currituck Inlet. A third would be stationed on the remote Smith's Island, at the mouth of the bay. A fourth would cover the beaches of Northampton County. And a fifth would serve as a lookout for the shore of Accomac. If the patrols spotted anything suspicious, they would immediately inform the local commander, and he would issue a general notice of possible pirate landings to all other county militia commanders, as well as send a full report to Governor Nicholson. The council would also warn Captain Aldred, who had miraculously retained his commission as captain of a guard ship, of "any Ship or Vessel yt shall be at Anchor or Cruising by the Capes, or upon ye Coast, if Suspected to be a pyrate."

In spite of these defensive measures, the aftermath of the invasion of the Chesapeake by the *Providence Galley* left little doubt as to the vulnerability of Virginia's extensive and poorly guarded coastline. The new defensive network put in place kept a vigilant eye on the ships passing in and out of the Chesapeake Bay throughout the summer, but the lookouts reported no suspicious activity.

In mid-October 1699, however, Colonel John Custis, commander of the Northampton County Militia, sent an urgent dispatch to Governor Nicholson informing him that a ship had anchored close to the beach near Smith's Island. Twelve men had come ashore and slaughtered several cattle, which they carried off before sailing away under cover of night. No one knew whether the thieves had put back out to sea or were making their way up the Chesapeake. Certain that the thieves must be from a pirate ship, Colonel Custis sent a squad of men to investigate.

Isolated, undefended, and without a militia to repel invaders if they chose to land along the Virginia coastline, Smith's Island was a favored location for pirate vessels in search of fresh water, foodstuffs, and timber. With these facts in mind, Custis suggested that the *Essex Prize* or some other guard ship be stationed in Smith's Island River, where the pirates would most likely bring their vessel for reprovisioning.

The entire question became moot, however, for the *Essex Prize* was scheduled to go up the Elizabeth River for a refit, or so Governor Nicholson said in a somewhat apologetic letter to Custis. The best the governor could promise was assistance when the ship was again seaworthy—whenever that might be.

Nicholson's inability to curtail piracy in Virginia again became obvious in the late fall when a pirate by the name of Henry King, once a Pennsylvania trader, seized and plundered the London merchantman *John Hopewell*, under the command of Captain Henry Munday, off the Virginia coast. The owners of the *John Hopewell* dispatched a letter to Governor Nicholson, dated November 1699, saying that in the encounter, nine of the ship's crewmen had signed on with pirate captain Henry King, and that if they should land in Virginia, the owners wanted them apprehended and brought to trial.

The governor insisted he was powerless to do anything, and the raiding would have continued unabated had it not been for the onset of winter. Shipping slowed and the pirates made their way south to the West Indies. But when spring returned to the Virginia coastline, so would the seaborne raiders.

As Governor Nicholson's long winter of discontent slowly warmed into spring, the miserable prospects of pirate invasions of Virginia's Chesapeake waters loomed like an impenetrable fog on the horizon. Captain Aldred and the *Essex Prize* were a sadly inadequate defense, and the colony was still living under the shadow of fear cast by the bold raids of the *Providence Galley* and her supposed consort. It seemed that only a miracle could protect the coasts and shipping of Virginia from the inevitable return of the pirates.

Then, on the balmy afternoon of April 20, 1700, that miracle appeared in the form of a sleek, powerful guardian: a thirty-two-gun man-of-war named HMS *Shoreham*. In the *Shoreham*, the Virginians might actually have a suitable protector against the impending pirate season that would plague the colony's shipping and commerce from spring through late autumn. The warship's arrival was none too soon, because close in her wake came the pirates.

Space does not allow us to go into the details of all the harrowing encounters that took place off the Virginia coast during the turbulent spring of 1700, but the battles, victories, and defeats are summarized in the following document, which can be found in the Colonial Records Project at the Library of Virginia:

Survey Report No. 4385

13 May 1700

This document contains 21 depositions sworn before the Court of Oyer & Terminer for the trial of pirates in Virginia before Peter Beverly, Clerk of Arraigns. Some of the depositions are sworn by individual mariners, others by groups of mariners from different ships captured by Lewis Guittar. All ships were

outward bound from Virginia, except the Pennsylvania Merchant, which was inbound from England.

On 17 April (1699) the BALTIMORE was captured; on 18 April
the GEORGE of Pennsylvania bound for Jamica. The master of
the FRIENDSHIP of Belfast-Hans Haniel-was killed when the
pirates fired on his ship.

On 28 April 4 ships were captured within the Cape of Virginia including the PENNSYLVANIA MERCHANT, and the INDIAN KING
of Virginia and the NICHOLSON. The PENNSYLVANIA MERCHANT was
burnt. The crews taken prisoner were confined in the hold of
the pirate ship which was call LA PAIX (PEACE); some other being
made to throw cargoes of tobacco and other goods to Lyn-
Haven by the pirates.

On 28 April Captain John Alread, Commander of H.M.S.
ESSEX having heard of the pirates' exploits came ashore and
informed H. E. Francis Nicholson H.M. Governor General of
Virginia and Captain Passenger of H.M.S. SHOREHAM that there
was a Pirate in Lyn-Haven Bay. Whereupon captain Passenger
and His Excellency, together with Captain Alread and Peter
Hayman Esquire, went aboard H.M.S. SHOREHAM and in coming
out of the James River engaged the Pirate ship. Captain Guittar
fought under a blood red flag. Peter Hayman Esquire was slain.
After an engagement which lasted 6 to 8 hours John Lympany,
a passenger from the PENNSYLVANIA MERCHANT, was ordered by
Lewis Guittar to swim aboard the SHOREHAM to inform H. E. the
Governor that there were English prisoners aboard his ship and
that they and the ship would be blown up unless H. E. was prepared to grant Quarter to Guittar and his men if they surrendered.

The Governor gave his promise. About 124 pirates were
taken prisoner and some 25 to 30 pirates were slain. Between
40 and 50 English prisoners were liberated.

Lewis Guittar

In December 1699, a tiny pirate sloop set sail from Hispaniola in the West Indies. The commander was a French buccaneer named Lewis Guittar, who had only recently been elected captain by the weary and disgruntled crew. His appointment as captain triggered a course of events that would bring him and his fractious crew into one of the bloodiest confrontations with the forces of law and order in the history of the Chesapeake Bay.

Within two weeks of assuming command, Guittar seized his first victim while cruising along the coast of Hispaniola. This prize was a small Dutch trading vessel carrying a cargo of linen for the Spanish trade. The pirates snapped up the defenseless merchant ship, and after plundering part of her cargo and a supply of brandy, they pressed her ship's surgeon into service. Then they released the ship and the rest of the crew to make their way with their remaining cargo.

The surgeon, whose name has been lost to history, proved significantly valuable to Guittar, for he claimed to have recently been cheated out of 600 or 700 crowns by the master of a Dutch merchantman engaged in trade with Suriname. He described the merchant vessel as an exceptional ship with superior sailing qualities and told the pirates its most likely whereabouts. His only desire, he claimed, was "to be revenged upon the Master of the Shipp who had wronged him." Guittar was excited at the possibility of capturing this fine sailing vessel for his own use and immediately charted an intercept course.

The vessel in question was named *La Paix* (Peace), which proved to be a rather ironic name for a ship that ultimately was used for violence, intimidation, and piracy. Guittar sailed to Saltitudos Island in the Barbados, where the vessel was thought to lie. They easily located *La Paix*, which surrendered without a fight. As promised, Guittar avenged the

69

wrongs done to his new surgeon by setting the ship's master, Captain Cornelius Isaac, adrift in a small rowboat.

La Paix was a large, sleek new vessel of about 200 tons, eighty-four feet in length, twenty-five feet abeam, and eleven feet deep in the hold. She possessed a single deck fore and aft, with a small forecastle and a half or quarterdeck extending to the mainmast. Significantly, she was also capable of wielding at least twenty guns, and once properly equipped and fitted, she would prove a formidable opponent to almost any ship plying the Caribbean trade routes. Guittar decided *La Paix* would become his new flagship.

To test the abilities and might of their new prize, Guittar and crew commenced a cruise of the West Indies during which they captured at least four ships. Every time they took a ship, they captured its supplies, provisions, and upgrades and added them to *La Paix*. Whenever a ship put up any resistance before being taken, Guittar ordered that a few of the defeated crewmen or officers should be hanged from their own yardarms as an example to the rest of the crew. Like many pirates before and after him, Guittar knew that terror and a fearsome reputation were highly effective weapons in the game of piracy. He offered some victims the opportunity of joining the freebooters serving under him, and those who refused this generous offer were frequently hanged, tortured, set adrift, or marooned. On other occasions, however, the pirates took, looted, and then released prizes with no harm or damage beyond being relieved of their goods and cargo. It would seem that quick capitulation to the pirates' demands fostered mercy, whereas any attempt to run or resist was severely punished when the pirates eventually took the ship. As victory piled on top of victory, *La Paix* grew in strength; the pirates continued to add armaments and improvements, and the crew increased in number.

On April 17, 1700, a 100-ton Bristol pink named *Baltimore*, commanded by Captain John Lovejoy, hove into view as she was en route from Barbados to Virginia. The pirates didn't much care what cargo she might be carrying; the *Baltimore* was a very desirable ship. The pink, a much faster sailing vessel than even *La Paix*, was the type of vessel virtually all pirates coveted, but in order to capture the *Baltimore*, Captain Guittar would first have to catch her. The race was on.

Guittar decided a ruse might help him capture the swift-running pink. *La Paix* hoisted Dutch colors and signal flags indicating that she was in distress and needed assistance. This lame-duck ruse led the unfortunate Captain Lovejoy to wait for *La Paix* to catch up to the *Baltimore*. As Guittar came alongside the *Baltimore*, he hailed her, inquiring as to her name, from whence she hailed, and where she was bound. Then, while Lovejoy was answering the questions, a pirate sharpshooter shot and killed one of the pink's passengers, a merchant named James Waters. Seeing that he was clearly outmatched and outwitted, Lovejoy immediately surrendered his unarmed vessel.

The pirates took Lovejoy and several other crewmen prisoner and clapped them in irons in the belly of *La Paix*. Guittar decided that although she was without armament, the *Baltimore* would make a fine, fast consort for *La Paix*, along with another old sloop they had taken previously. Guittar sent his quartermaster and several others aboard the *Baltimore* to take command, and then he ordered the *Baltimore* to follow him closely. The tropical climate of the West Indies was already growing oppressive, even though it was still springtime, so the three ships set a course for Virginia. If they became separated, they planned to meet up at a specified rendezvous point, but Guittar strictly ordered the *Baltimore* "to attend upon them till they were within the Capes" of Virginia. In Virginia, the pirates could take on fresh water and provisions, and the weary crewmen would be able to find some relaxation and revelry . . . or at least, that was the plan.

About a hundred leagues from Virginia, *La Paix* and the *Baltimore* encountered the sloop *George*, bound from Pennsylvania to Jamaica under the command of Captain Joseph Forrest. The pirates captured and plundered the *George* immediately, removing her cargo even while they were still taking her crew aboard the three pirate vessels. Deeming the prize unworthy of the manpower required to keep her, Guittar ordered his men to bore holes in her hull and set her ablaze.

The next day, the pirates had arrived within thirty leagues of Cape Henry when they sighted a fat, slow-moving Virginia-bound brigantine named the *Barbados Merchant*. The pirates charted an intercept course and gave chase. The *Baltimore*, by far the fastest of the three pirate ships, rapidly outdistanced the flagship and came up alongside the *Barbados Merchant* alone. Although the pink carried no cannons, she had a crew of sixty pirates, all of whom were armed with pistols, pikes, cutlasses, and muskets and would have little trouble overwhelming the crew of the brigantine. In a bit of pirate glory for the former quartermaster of *La Paix*, the *Barbados Merchant* surrendered without a fight.

In keeping with previously established protocol, when *La Paix* caught up with the *Baltimore* and the captured prize, they treated her captain, William Fletcher, and crew with respect out of consideration for her cooperation and quick surrender. The pirates plundered the ship while they kept Captain Fletcher and his men in respectful custody on the deck of *La Paix*. Some of the pirates tried to persuade the crew of the *Barbados Merchant* to cast their lots with the buccaneers by luring them with tales of riches far beyond what they could ever hope to earn aboard a merchantman. But when the brigantine's crewmen remained loyal to their captain, their refusal soured the otherwise cordial atmosphere of the encounter, and the mood of the pirates became increasingly vicious. History does not record the conversation between the merchants and the pirates, but it must have been harsh and insulting, because the pirates seized Captain Fletcher, stripped him of his clothing, and savagely beat him with the flat of a cutlass. They likely would have beaten him to death had not one of the buccaneers apparently interceded on his behalf.

This harsh demonstration "persuaded" at least a carpenter and one of the brigantine sailors to sign the articles of piracy, while the remainder of the crew still steadfastly refused. Enraged and insulted, the pirates began vandalizing the *Barbados Merchant*, smashing her compass, cutting away her rudder, and stealing every last candle and lantern aboard, as well as cutting down her masts, sails, and bowsprit and casting them into the Atlantic. In a vindictive fury, they removed all the charts, papers, books, maps, food, water, and even the longboat. The pirates then sailed away, leaving the crew of the *Barbados Merchant* adrift in a leaking hulk with no food, water, sails, oars, or means of navigation. Floating aimlessly, they would face a slow, inevitable, and agonizing death at sea.

But the departure of Guittar and his crew had been slightly too hasty. In their orgy of destruction and vandalism, the pirates failed to notice that the foremast and sails that they had cut away were still hanging over the side of the ship in a tangled mess. The fact that the section of mast and sail was tethered to the rails had prevented it from sinking into the depths of the Atlantic. The merchant sailors hoisted the fragments aboard and cobbled together a sad-looking but functional repair job. Meanwhile, Captain Fletcher managed to locate an antique pocket compass that the pirates had overlooked in their general destruction and plundering, and the crippled vessel struggled along under a full moon and eventually limped toward the port at Accomac on the Chesapeake Bay.

As the pirates made their way toward the Virginia coastline, the *Baltimore* sailed well ahead of *La Paix* and the consort sloop. Guittar plotted a course "to make the best of his way for the Capes [and] might a light for the pink to follow." But the pink, for whatever reason, took no notice. Perhaps her crewmen had not seen the command sent by the flagship, or perhaps having tasted victory in single-handedly capturing the *Barbados Merchant*, they had designs of their own. We will probably never know why, but what we do know is that she sailed off on her own—too fast to follow—and Guittar never saw the pink again.

By the morning of April 23, 1700, *La Paix* was about twenty leagues off the coast of Cape Henry with her consort sloop when her crew spied a brigantine named the *Pennsylvania Merchant*, captained by Samuel Harrison and bound for Philadelphia from England. The wind had died and all three ships lay nearly becalmed. By afternoon, however, a slight sea breeze picked up just about the time Captain Harrison spied *La Paix* flying Dutch colors and accompanied by a small sloop. As *La Paix* maneuvered to take the weather gauge, her evil intentions became clear and the *Pennsylvania Merchant* made a run for it—at least insofar as the slight breeze would grant any of the ships mobility. What began as a nerve-shattering, slow-motion chase picked up speed as the afternoon turned to evening and a freshening breeze skimmed across the water, filling the ships' sails.

Sailing north with the pirates following in close pursuit, the *Pennsylvania Merchant* crossed paths with and hailed the pathetically crippled *Barbados Merchant* as her crew desperately tried to make their way to land. The crew of the *Pennsylvania Merchant* shouted that they would stop to help if they had the time, but they were being chased. Captain Fletcher, aboard the battered and broken *Barbados Merchant*, shouted back that they were right to be afraid of their pursuers and should run for their lives. But the delay caused by Harrison's slowing down to hail Fletcher was enough for the pirates to gain ground on their fleeing target. As dusk began to settle, the pirates pulled close to the merchantman's stern and ordered her to surrender.

Harrison reportedly shouted defiantly to the shadowy craft, "Keep off or I will open fire." Guittar apparently was unwilling to undertake a boarding action on a night when the moon was totally covered by clouds, so he stood off from his prey, lurking nearby. Harrison sailed through the night, trying to elude the predators, but Guittar and his consort shadowed the ship's every move. As morning broke, the soft dawn light showed the brigantine and the pirates' flagship within striking range of each other. Guittar again demanded that the merchant vessel surrender and fired a cannon across her bow. Harrison later remarked, "I did not think the [pirate] Shipp had been so big over night." But in the early light of dawn, he was awed by the size and firepower of *La Paix*. The *Pennsylvania Merchant* immediately surrendered, and the pirates ordered Harrison aboard their ship. Guittar demanded to know why they had run all night rather than surrender when they first encountered. Harrison innocently replied, "Because there was peace with all the world."

Boats began to ferry plunder back and forth between the vessels. The pirates stripped the crew members of all their clothing and treated them roughly in retaliation for their nighttime defiance. The brigantine also carried thirty-one passengers, who were making their way to the colonies from England, and the pirates systematically robbed them of everything they owned. One of them, a man named Joseph Wood, was carrying 900 pounds sterling in cash and 360 pounds in bonds and papers—though the pirates probably had no idea what the papers were, other than that they were official-looking documents or commissions with seals and patents. Additionally, the pirates stripped sails, rigging, tackle, apparel, and other goods from the ship and ferried them to *La Paix*. The plunder of the *Pennsylvania Merchant* totaled several thousand pounds in cash and cargo.

The pirates informed Harrison that they intended to burn his ship as punishment for having inconvenienced them with his evasive overnight chase. The real reason, however, was more likely that Guittar knew that releasing the prize so close to Virginia would give Harrison the opportunity to inform one of the official Virginia guardships of the whereabouts of *La Paix*. His ship was strong and fast, but Guittar had no desire to test her against a British man-of-war.

Harrison begged the pirates to release him, along with his ship, crewmen, and passengers. The pirates said they would put the matter to a vote, but predictably, they decided that the *Pennsylvania Merchant* should be burned. They first moved all crewmen and passengers to the pirate ships, and then a pirate named John Houghling, who had been with *La Paix* since before Guittar captured her, was sent aboard the *Pennsylvania Merchant* to start a fire. Entering Captain Harrison's cabin, Houghling built a fire as another pirate forced the merchant ship's carpenter to cut a hole in her side. The grinning Houghling returned to *La Paix* wearing one of Harrison's coats as well as a pair of his stockings and boots. The pirates set the *Pennsylvania Merchant* adrift, ablaze and sinking, while they took her captain, crew, and passengers below deck and imprisoned them with the growing number of other captives confined in the holds.

Brimming with cargo and prisoners, the pirate convoy set sail to the south and neared the Virginia Capes on the morning of April 28, intent on refitting and provisioning their ships. As they sailed inbound, they spotted two merchantmen outward bound from the Chesapeake. These were the *Indian King*, a beautiful Virginia-built vessel commanded by Captain Edward Whitaker and headed to London, and the smaller *Friendship*, bound for Liverpool with a cargo of tobacco. Guittar was unable to resist the temptation of such easy prey, and *La Paix* set after the larger vessel. As the pirate ship approached, the merchant vessels tried to flee, but it was too late. Guittar hoisted "his Bloody Ensign" and fired a warning shot at the *Indian King*. She immediately surrendered, and a boarding party scrambled onto her decks, taking the captain, mate, surgeon, crew, and passengers captive and binding their hands behind them. In a now familiar scene, some of the pirates trundled their prisoners aboard *La Paix*, where they robbed them of their personal possessions, while others pillaged and plundered the freshly loaded and provisioned ship of all her valuables and cargo.

While he welcomed the plunder and booty, what Guittar really wanted was information. He interrogated Captain Whitaker regarding Virginia and its maritime defenses, specifically demanding to know whether any men-of-war were prowling the waters of the Chesapeake. Whitaker was entirely unaware of the arrival of HMS *Shoreham*, which had been sent to Virginia for that very purpose, and reported that only the *Essex Prize* protected the Chesapeake. "I told him," he later recalled, "that there was none that I knew of, Except a Smalle One [and] I hearde that she was gone to home." Guittar was pleased by this news and pressed his captives for information about valuables and goods aboard both the *Indian King* and the still uncaptured *Friendship*.

Guittar locked Whitaker, his crew, and passengers below deck with his other captives and set off in pursuit of the *Friendship*. Around ten o'clock, *La Paix* bore down on the *Friendship* and unleashed a volley of small-arms fire with muskets and pistols. Her captain, Hans Hammil, was near the mizzenmast when he was shot through the head in the volley of bullets. The ship's crew immediately struck her sails and gave her up to be boarded. The pirates ordered the ship's mate, John Calwell, to come aboard their ship. When he and four other crewmen from the *Friendship* arrived on deck, they were met by Captain Lewis Guittar and pilot John Houghling.

Guittar asked if anyone had been killed. Calwell replied that the master of the ship had been shot. Amazingly, Guittar appeared genuinely sorry and offered to send his best surgeon over to attend to the captain. Calwell bitterly and mournfully told him that it was too late. Hougling stepped forward, feigning sympathy, and inquired in mock consolation where the captain had been standing when he fell. "By the mizzen shrouds," replied Calwell. "Wrong," corrected the pilot, starting to laugh boastfully. "He stood beside the Mizen Mast and I fired the Gun that Shott him." And with that he burst into a wild, insane laughter and walked away.

The pirates confined the *Friendship*'s crew below deck and then plundered their ship, as they had done to so many other ships before. With two new prizes in tow, La Paix sailed into the Chesapeake. As they entered Lynnhaven Bay, they came upon several ships floating at anchor. Guittar asked one of his prisoners, Captain Whitaker, if he knew whether any of the anchored vessels were merchantmen. Whitaker had no idea, so Guittar selected one of the finer-looking ships and bore down on her. She was the *Nicholson* and was under the command of Robert Lurtine, soon to depart for London with a cargo of seven hundred hogsheads of tobacco. As the pirate ship came alongside the *Nicholson* and into speaking range, Lurtine hailed the approaching stranger in a friendly fashion, asking from which port she sailed. The pirates on deck drew their pistols and shouted, "Out of the Sea you Doggs," before unleashing a volley of shot.

The *Nicholson* had been preparing to depart when the pirates entered the bay, and now she quickly slipped her mooring line and unfurled her sails to make a run for the open ocean. The pirates came about and pursued the fleeing merchantman for hours. Though the *Nicholson* was a swift sailing vessel, *La Paix*'s crew managed to keep the ship from escaping and eventually maneuvered close enough to fire her cannons. After hours of dogged pursuit punctuated by occasional strikes by cannonballs and shot, the pirates had shot away the *Nicholson*'s mainyard and main topsail, and further flight was becoming impossible. Lurtine struck his colors and came to before the pirates damaged his ship beyond repair or killed any more of his crewmen.

Pleased with himself, Guittar positioned his flagship to capture his prize. So intent was his focus on the *Nicholson* that he apparently did not notice the small, swift pink whose crew had witnessed the attack and were now hurriedly making their way up the James River on a mission to alert the authorities.

Guittar found the *Nicholson* every bit as desirable as she had seemed from a distance. She was fast and maneuverable, and she could readily be converted to suit his needs. She would be a lovely addition to his growing armada and would make a suitable replacement for the pink that had deserted him. But to convert the *Nicholson* into a pirate vessel, his men would have to clear some of the deck to make room for cannons and empty the hold of all those hogsheads of tobacco to make room for other booty, as well as prisoners. Guittar sent a large number of crewmen aboard to take possession of his new prize and make her ready as an escort, but their alterations were delayed by the discovery of a large supply of "strong Beere and some Red Wine on board," which the pirates seized and began drinking.

Perhaps not surprisingly, the more they drank, the more belligerent and cruel they became. Apparently as punishment for resisting capture, they bound several members of the *Nicholson*'s crew and beat them nearly senseless while continuously interrogating them. While being subjected to this torture, the *Nicholson*'s carpenter insisted that there was a man-of-war in the area. Captain Whitaker had previously told them that there was no man-of-war, so the pirates removed a flint from a musket lock and began cranking the fastening screw into the carpenter's thumb. Once the makeshift thumbscrew had bored its way entirely through the man's thumb, they proceeded to beat him with the flats of their cutlasses and "told him he should not lye the next time."

While some of the pirates continued with their brutal sport, others forced the prisoners aboard *La Paix* to transfer sails, provisions, and armaments from the *Indian King* to the *Nicholson*. Meanwhile, still others compelled the crew of the *Nicholson* at sword and pistol point to work through the night dumping their valuable cargo of tobacco overboard. By dawn, 112 hogsheads of tobacco were floating on the tide. Many of the pirates by this time had drunk themselves into a stupor, but sobriety would come quicker than they expected.

That evening, April 28, a massive man-of-war called the *Shoreham*, under a Captain Passenger, made her way down the James River. Captain Whitaker, the *Indian King*'s former commander, spotted her silent approach and taunted Captain Guittar with the news that there "was a great Shipp" on the move. Guittar scoffed at the information, saying that he knew for a fact that there were no men-of-war in the vicinity. The only protection afforded to the Chesapeake and the entirety of the coast of Virginia was the decrepit *Essex Prize*, he said, and her captain was both incompetent and a coward. If, in fact, Whitaker had sighted a large ship, then Guittar thought she was far more likely to be a merchantman. And if she was a large merchantman with a full cargo . . . he would take her as yet another prize. The *Nicholson*'s unfortunate carpenter also warned Guittar of the approaching man-of-war, but again the pirate captain arrogantly chose to ignore the information. While Guittar and his men were feeling invincible, Captain Passenger and the men of the *Shoreham* kept a safe distance and spent the night preparing for a dawn battle.

When the morning sun began to illuminate the water, it became apparent that the "great Shipp" waiting a few miles distant was indeed a man-of-war. All the pirates who had been scattered through the flotilla, storing provisions and rigging sails, were summoned back to the flagship. The urgency of situation undoubtedly served to sober up the vast majority of the overindulgent pirates, but two of them, Cornelius Frank and François Delaunee, were sleeping off their drunkenness in the captain's and first mate's cabins aboard the *Nicholson*. The pirates drove nearly fifty of the prisoners aboard *La Paix* below deck and locked them in the cramped fore hold, where they remained in claustrophobic darkness throughout the ensuing battle.

Knowing that he could not hope to outgun the mighty *Shoreham*, Guittar devised a plan. He would sail to the windward side of the man-of-war, pull close in, and board her in the hope that she might be lightly crewed and his seasoned pirates could overwhelm her crew members in hand-to-hand combat. The pirates loosed *La Paix*'s topsails and hoisted the Jolly Roger. Captain Passenger bore down on her and fired a shot across her bow as a demand for surrender. The pirates replied by unleashing a broadside against the *Shoreham*, after which they tried to get to windward, but the *Shoreham* moved to cut them off. They tried again and again, but the man-of-war sailed well and prevented *La Paix* from getting the wind to her advantage. Meanwhile, broadside after broadside boomed up the Chesapeake as the two ships closed within musket range, fired, and separated before closing again and again.

As it happened, Guittar's supposition about the *Shoreham*'s crew proved correct. Having set out in a hurry, the *Shoreham* did not have a large enough crew to simultaneously sail the ship and man the guns, and the crew largely consisted of young recruits and hastily assembled volunteers from nearby merchant vessels. Although the *Shoreham* could not manage a constant rate of fire, her massive ranks of thirty-two guns had a withering effect on the pirates when they were unleashed. Both sides suffered damage and casualties, but the fight continued relentlessly. Neither Captain Passenger nor Lewis Guittar was going to back down from the confrontation.

For hours the pirates tried vainly to catch the wind and outmaneuver the warship, but without success. Damage on the crowded decks of *La Paix* bordered on carnage: masts, yards, rigging, and sails were shredded "all to shatters," several of the deck guns had pulled free of their carriages, and her hull was badly battered and leaking. Guittar knew it was only a matter of time before he was forced to draw out of range and disengage, or he would lose the ability to catch the wind and control his ship. He sailed up along the nearest shore and swung his helm hard to leeward, but nothing happened; the ship's rudder had been blown away. With tattered sails, splintered masts, tangled rigging, and no rudder, *La Paix* was drifting aimlessly. The pursuing *Shoreham* showered the pirate ship's deck with grapeshot, driving the pirates below deck to avoid being torn to pieces. Hiding below deck, they were unable to make the necessary repairs to control their ship, and eventually *La Paix* foundered and ran aground. Captain Passenger brought the *Shoreham* to anchor nearby and waited. Around four o'clock that afternoon, Guittar lowered the blood-red pirate flag and hoisted a white flag of surrender.

It seemed nearly over for Lewis Guittar. His ship was disabled and he had no means of escape, but he did have one last hand to play. He had fifty prisoners in his hold, and his men had vowed to live or die together. The pirates insisted they would rather blow up the ship with everyone aboard than dance the hangman's jig in Virginia. A trail of shiny, black powder connected no less than thirty barrels of gunpowder as Guittar informed his captive guests of his intentions. The prisoners, led by Captain Lurtrine of the *Nicholson*, begged the pirates to allow one of their number to swim over to HMS *Shoreham* and inform her captain and crew of their plight. One of them, Baldwin Mathews, agreed to go and dived overboard. Instead of swimming to the *Shoreham*, however, he swam as fast as he could for the beach.

A second volunteer named John Lumpany, who had been a passenger aboard the *Pennsylvania Merchant*, approached Guittar. As he later described it: "The Capt. Of the Pyrates bid me have good courage and speake to this Effect. Tell the Commander in chief if he will not give me and my men Quarter and Pardon I will blow the Shipp up and we will all dye together." Lumpany duly dived into the Chesapeake and swam to the *Shoreham*, where he delivered the terms of surrender to Virginia's Governor Nicholson, who had been with Captain Passenger when news of the pirates had arrived and had climbed aboard the new warship assigned to protect the Chesapeake.

The governor responded promptly with a note in his own hand, which read: "Whereas Capt Lewis [Guittar] Commander of the Lay Paste [*sic*] hath proffered to surrender himselfe, men and Ship together with what effects thereunto belongeth provided he may have quarter which I grant him on performance of the same and referr him and his men to the mercy of my Royal Master King William the third whom God preserve." Captain Lewis Guittar accepted the terms and surrendered his crew and his flagship, *La Paix*. The battle was over.

Several sailors aboard *La Paix* jumped overboard in an attempt to escape capture. According to witnesses who had gathered to watch the battle, at least five or six men dived into the rolling surf, but only one of them made it to shore alive. When questioned by some of the witnesses, he said that he was from New York and had been taken captive and pressed into service aboard the pirate vessel. He told the witnesses that they should all run, because the pirates intended to blow up the ship. Some of them ran frantically into the forest, but when others saw the New Yorker fleeing the scene, they chased him down and apprehended him. It turned out that he was none other than the brutal pirate John Houghling.

Aboard the *Shoreham*, the battle had been costly. The fine new ship was damaged, four men had been killed, and many more were wounded. But on *La Paix*, the damage was far, far greater. Of the 150 or so pirates aboard, 26 had been killed in the battle and another fifteen had been so seriously wounded that eight of them died of their wounds over the next several weeks. Captain Passenger took 124 pirates prisoner and turned them over to the militia of Elizabeth City County to await shipment to London, where they would face trial before the king's justice. But three of Guittar's men would not have the benefit of the clemency afforded by the terms of surrender, as they were not aboard *La Paix* at the time of surrender. These men were John Houghling, who had been captured onshore, as well as Cornelius Frank and François Delaunee, the drunken pirates who were out cold on the *Nicholson* through the entire battle. All three were subsequently hanged.

Samuel "Black Sam" Bellamy and Palsgrave Williams

Samuel Bellamy and Palsgrave (or Paul) Williams were typical of the pirates, brigands, and buccaneers who terrorized the Chesapeake Bay in the early eighteenth century. It is thought that Samuel Bellamy was born on March 18, 1689, in Devonshire, England, the son of Stephen and Elizabeth Pain Bellamy. He was the youngest of five children, the eldest son having died in infancy five years before Samuel's birth. As the only living son, he stood to inherit the family farm, which probably didn't amount to much. His home village was an extremely modest place, consisting of only a handful of cottages scattered across a hill on the northern fringe of the stark wastes of Dartmoor. Not relishing a life trying to eke out a subsistence from the hard clay soil of his land, Bellamy left the farm as soon as he could to escape the social and economic catastrophe engulfing the English countryside as a result of "enclosure" laws restricting the use of land.

Plenty of people were trying to lure young men like Sam Bellamy aboard their ships. Professional seamen were in short supply, and the captains of both merchant vessels and Royal Navy warships were continually shorthanded. By some estimates, even if every English sailor had been healthy and working at the same time, they would have supplied only about two-thirds of the manpower needed for the empire's merchant and naval fleets. Consequently, both services actively courted volunteers—the navy offered a bounty of two months' pay to anyone who would sign up—but they got few takers. There was a saying that "those who would go to sea for pleasure would go to hell as a pastime." Only the ignorant and naïve joined either service voluntarily. Sam Bellamy had been raised on tales of the exploits of the notorious pirate Henry Avery, however, who hailed from a town only thirty miles from the Bellamy farm and managed to retire unscathed with his booty. The few country boys who, like Sam, were itching for adventure were snapped up quickly by naval recruiters and the dreaded press gangs that shanghaied the unwary, making them virtual slaves on Royal Navy ships.

The onset of the War of the Spanish Succession in 1701 caused further changes in Sam Bellamy's life. He was a thirteen-year-old ship's boy on a merchant vessel when the conflict began, and by the time it ended, he was a skilled mariner, able to guide a vessel a thousand miles and handle grappling hooks, firearms, and cannon. Sometime between 1713 and 1715, young Sam arrived in Boston, where most inbound ships cleared customs before proceeding to other New England ports.

With a population of just over ten thousand residents, Boston was the largest city in British North America, and the port through which most transatlantic commerce of the northeastern seaboard passed. Bellamy's ship would have docked at the end of Long Wharf, a newly completed pier jutting sixteen hundred feet into the harbor, providing dock space for thirty or more oceangoing vessels to tie up simultaneously in water deep enough that their crews could unload their cargoes directly onto the docks at either high or low tide.

According to legend, Bellamy took to hanging around the taproom of an Eastham, Massachusetts, tavern. One spring night in 1715, he met a sixteen-year-old girl named Mary or Maria Hallett, charming her with tales of his maritime adventures. Sam and Mary had a roll in the hay the very night they met, and in most versions of the story, they were sufficiently smitten with each other to begin talking of marriage. But Mary's parents were wealthy farmers and refused to allow their daughter to marry a penniless sailor, whom they considered the lowest of the low. Sam was furious and vowed that he would make his fortune and return to claim his bride.

After Sam returned to sea in September of 1715, the terrified girl discovered she was pregnant, and later that winter she supposedly was found in a barn with a dead infant in her arms. The good people of Eastham, who were Puritan descendants of the Pilgrims, subjected Mary to a public whipping before tossing her into the town jail to await trial for her infant's murder. By some accounts, she went mad during her incarceration and, with the possible assistance of the devil, escaped to live a hermit's life on the stark tablelands above the Atlantic shoreline. There she roamed, scaring children, furtively scanning the horizon for her lost love's ship, and bringing nasty storms to plague passing sailors—hobbies that earned her the epithet Sea Witch of Billingsgate (the old name for the north end of Boston now known as Wellfleet).

While this colorful story has all the makings of legend and folktale, we know that a young girl named Mary Hallett indeed lived in Eastham in 1715, and the course of her life closely followed the legend. Whatever the truth about Mary Hallett, we do know that Sam Bellamy made another, more lasting acquaintance while in New England: a man named Palsgrave or Paul Williams.

Williams was thirty-nine years old when he met the younger Bellamy. He was a silversmith from an influential Rhode Island family, with a wife and two young boys at home. At first glance, Williams would have seemed a most unlikely pirate. His father, John Williams, was the attorney general of Rhode Island and an exceptionally wealthy merchant who split his time between a Boston mansion and estates in Newport and Block Island. His mother, Anna Alcock, was a descendant of the Plantagenet kings of England and the daughter of a Harvard-trained physician. Yet their son chose the life of an outlaw, joining a society of impoverished mariners who were fighting to gain the wealth and freedom that he had already been enjoying since birth. It makes no sense—until you take his stepfather and childhood neighbors into account.

John Williams died in 1687, when his son was eleven years old, leaving the execution of his will and the guardianship of his children in the hands of a friend, a Scottish exile named Robert Guthrie. Guthrie married Palsgrave's mother a year and a half later, permanently settling the family on their estate on Block Island in Rhode Island's Narragansett Bay, a move that profoundly altered the trajectory of young Paul's life. Guthrie's father had been a famous nationalist and preacher in Scotland who had been executed by the English in front of his family while Guthrie was still an infant. Guthrie's mother and siblings were banished from the country, joining a large contingent of Scottish prisoners of war transported to New England to slave in the ironworks at the towns of Lynn and Braintree, Massachusetts.

On Block Island, Guthrie—and by extension, the entire Williams family—became connected with some of the leading smugglers, money launderers, and black marketers in New England. Paul's eldest sister, Mary, married Edward Sands, a friend of Captain Kidd's, and the couple helped hide some of Kidd's contraband at their home while he was on the run from the law. Paul Williams may have become inclined to pursue illegal ventures through this complicit upbringing, and he undoubtedly romanticized the idea of an adventurous life of piracy, as children tend to do. But he needed a willing partner, someone who knew more than he did about sailing ships and navigation.

Hence, Sam Bellamy and Paul Williams became fast friends and formed a partnership. With his wealth and connections, Williams became the senior partner, able to secure supplies and a seaworthy vessel for use in their proposed maritime undertakings. Bellamy brought the skills of a mariner and a sound knowledge of the West Indies. According to their agreement, if Williams hired Bellamy to be the master of his vessel, Williams was entitled to shares of the profits of whatever commercial or smuggling scheme Bellamy was contemplating. But any plans the pair were hatching went out the window when news of a far greater opportunity arrived.

On July 13, 1715, a Spanish treasure fleet left Havana, Cuba, bound for Cadiz. Because of the War of the Spanish Succession, which had only recently ended, it had been several years since the Spanish had been able to dispatch their treasure fleets to the New World, so the galleons were carrying an unusually massive haul: coins, silks, porcelain, ingots of gold and silver, and jewels worth an estimated seven million pieces of eight (equivalent to 1,750,000 pounds sterling at the time). They were also departing unusually late in the season and risked facing the fury of Atlantic winter storms.

The eleven-ship armada sailed out of Havana and into the Florida Straits, their sails full and flags waving. Massive fighting galleons took the lead, their raised aft decks towering above both the main deck and the ocean waves like wooden skyscrapers. Six treasure galleons made up the body of the fleet, their hulls riding low in the water, laden with their precious cargo. A French frigate, more nimble than her fortresslike consorts, darted back and forth as a protective outrider. Two more fighting galleons brought up the rear, bristling with dozens of heavy bronze cannons. No pirate in his right mind would dare challenge such a formidable force. But no pirates would need to. As the flotilla approached the Florida Keys, a massive hurricane moved in, and the entire fleet sank in a scant thirty to fifty feet of water.

Fewer than half of the two thousand men aboard the doomed ships made it to the beaches alive, crawling in terror through the sting-ing rain, howling wind, and impenetrable darkness to shelter amid the dunes. Dozens more died from their wounds and dehydration while they huddled on the beach for days, watching for hostile Semi-nole Indians. While most of the ships' captains had perished in the storm, the admiral of the treasure fleet survived, took command of the survivors, and put them to work digging for water and building crude shelters from the wreckage of their ships that had washed onto the shore. Several men made their way toward St. Augustine in one of the ships' rowboats that had survived the wreckage; when they arrived a week later, they broke the news of one of the greatest maritime disas-ters in the history of the Americas. Along with the remains of ten ships and a thousand corpses, seven million pesos in treasure lay scattered off the beaches of east Florida, most of it in water so shallow a good diver could recover it without difficulty.

News of the disaster spread across the Americas like wildfire. Ship captains and crews carried the word to Charleston, Williamsburg, Newport, and Boston and from St. Augustine to Havana to Jamaica and the Bahamas. The *Boston News-Letter* did the rest, its late summer editions carried far and wide by ships, sloops, and post riders alerting readers from Cape Cod to London of the disaster. Soon, from every corner of British America, men were piling onto vessels of all sorts, bound "to fish upon ye wrecks." It was, in every sense of the word, America's first gold rush.

For Williams and Bellamy, it was a dream opportunity. Sometime in the early fall of 1715, they headed for the Florida wreck sites. Per-haps there were tearful good-byes between Sam and Mary Hallett, and between Paul and his wife, Anna, and their two children. When the two men eventually returned to New England, it would be under far different circumstances.

When news of the wreck of the Spanish treasure fleet reached Jamaica, all hell broke loose. Every mariner in town seemed to be readying himself to sail off to claim his share of the Spanish gold. Salvagers and divers arrived in the Florida Keys like vultures picking over a rotting carcass. The Spanish hired all the men they could to help recover their loot, but not surprisingly, once these men started bringing up gold, silver, and jewels worth several lifetimes of wages, they were unwilling to hand it over to the Spanish in exchange for a paltry paycheck. The divers and salvagers took off with their rescued treasure, turning outlaw, and even honest men became pirates as the hordes of mariners fought to pick clean the sunken wrecks.

Bellamy and Williams, deeply tanned, their hair bleached from months under the tropical sun, most likely arrived at the Spanish wrecks in early January 1716. The work was hard, dangerous, and competitive. By the end of the month, seven or eight other English vessels had anchored nearby, carrying others who intended to dive to the scattered wreckage of the same ship Sam and Paul were trying to loot. None of them, however, could locate the main hull section of the ship with its bulging cargo hold. Instead, they had to content themselves with odd bits of cargo and coins they found strewn across the ocean floor. After weeks of work, the wreckers had scrounged only five thousand to six thousand pieces of eight (worth 1,250 to 1,500 pounds sterling) to divide among the hundreds of men who crewed all the ships. By the end of January, the Spanish arrived with reinforcements from Havana and drove off the English-speaking salvage divers. Bellamy and Williams were probably happy to be sent away, but Bellamy could not bear the thought of returning empty-handed to New England and his beloved Mary. If he intended to make his fortune, he would have to follow the examples of the other wreckers and turn pirate.

Bellamy and Williams now made their way south, past the tip of Florida and the western end of Cuba, on down to the shores of Central America and the Bay of Honduras, where they had little trouble finding men willing to become pirates. By late March, the pair of salvagers-turned-pirates were heading a band operating out of a couple *periaguas*, a type of sailing canoe. Somewhere in the Bay of Honduras, they boarded their first known prize, a Dutch vessel commanded by John

Cornelison. The pirates looted the vessel and forced at least one sailor to join them under threat of death. Shortly thereafter, they seized control of an English sloop commanded by a Captain Young. While their men searched the ship for valuables, Bellamy and Williams tied their periaguas astern and forced Captain Young to take them back to Cuba.

Unlike many men who became sea robbers, Sam Bellamy and Paul Williams had no illusions of being privateers. They were opportunists who attacked indiscriminately, taking whatever wealthy prize they discovered. Like many of his breed, Bellamy had little sympathy for the ship owners and captains who had once made his life so miserable. He argued that the band should act like Robin Hood's men, taking from the wealthy merchants and enriching the poor sailors. Williams, already a wealthy merchant, chose to remain silent on the subject.

Off the coast of Cuba, Bellamy and Williams spotted four British sloops, under the command of a Captain Jennings, sailing into view and bearing down on them. Jennings was a known pirate hunter. Fearing capture, the pirates decided to make a run for it. They ordered their forty or so crewmen into the periaguas along with as much of the cargo and valuables as they could carry. As Jennings's flagship came alongside, Bellamy's gang jumped into the canoes, cast off the lines, and began rowing as hard as they could directly into the wind.

From the deck of his ship, Jennings watched the periaguas cast off but knew there was little point in pursuing them. Tacking against the wind, his sloops wouldn't be able to catch them before they made it into the reefs protecting the Cuban shoreline. Instead, he came alongside the sloop and hailed its master, Captain Young. Young assumed that these were some of Governor Hamilton's privateers, there to fight pirates and protect merchants like him, and he explained that the people in the two sailing canoes "were a parcel of villains" and had just made off with all his money.

As Bellamy and Williams escaped into the wind, they watched the English pirate hunters board Captain Young's sloop for the inevitable consultation between captains, but what happened next puzzled them. Young was clearly a legitimate trader, but instead of letting him go, the privateers put a prize crew aboard and took her along with them. Now, hidden among the reefs and mangrove swamps, Bellamy and Williams watched the little flotilla anchor at the entrance to Bahia Honda. The pirates in the periaguas realized that the men operating the sloops were not acting like sheriffs at all. For Bellamy, it confirmed that there was no law—at least no law that he could recognize. There was only force and fear and intimidation. It was a lesson that would serve him well.

Soon thereafter, Bellamy and Williams met up with the legendary buccaneer Captain Benjamin Hornigold. When the three met face-to-face off the coast of Cuba, Hornigold saw promise in the fledgling pirates and offered them membership in his band of sea raiders. After they read and signed the pirate articles, Bellamy and Williams joined the crew of the *Benjamin*, under the command of Captain Hornigold.

Mariners appreciate competence, and Sam Bellamy must have inspired a great deal of it, for despite his youth, Hornigold soon appointed him acting captain of the newly captured *Marianne*, advancing him ahead of several older men in his own crew—including Edward Teach, who later became the infamous Blackbeard. Sam and Paul now had a well-built oceangoing sloop at their disposal, a chest of treasure in the hold, and the most infamous English pirate of the day as their consort.

But by early July 1716, relations between the pirate companies were becoming strained. Hornigold's rule over the little squadron was failing as a result of his reluctance to attack English or Dutch ships. He imagined himself a privateer and held a fierce nationalistic loyalty toward his British homeland and her allies. He felt that he was something of a vigilante, settling old scores with the French and Spanish, and boarding friendly vessels only as a last resort to acquire vital supplies or skilled crewmen. Bellamy and Williams thought differently, and Captain Olivier Levasseur—a French pirate nicknamed La Buse (The Buzzard), with whom the rovers had teamed up—didn't see any reason not to attack English shipping along with any other prey that sailed their way.

While Hornigold was away in the Bahamas, Bellamy and La Buse teamed up to attack and capture several English vessels off the southern coast of Cuba, seizing men, provisions, and liquor. Upon his return, Hornigold was furious at their choice of targets. In the steaming heat of a Caribbean August, tensions reached a boiling point. Bellamy and La Buse wanted to plunder an English vessel sailing nearby, but Hornigold again refused. Aboard Hornigold's ship, the *Adventure*, many of the crewmen called for a vote to relieve him of his command, claiming that their commander was overlooking valuable prizes because of an outdated sense of patriotic loyalty. Perhaps younger, hungrier, more radical leadership was in order. The quartermaster called for a vote of the ship's company. Hornigold lost the confidence of two-thirds of the crew; the majority wanted no-holds-barred piracy and decided to join Bellamy and La Buse aboard their ships.

The speed of Samuel Bellamy's ascent to power was remarkable, even for a pirate. Only one year after leaving New England as a penniless, twenty-year-old sailor, he had become the commodore of a band of nearly two hundred pirates. He and Williams had already taken thousands of pounds' worth of cargo and gold, far more than he and all of his fellow sailors ever could have hoped to earn in a lifetime of legitimate service. Sam Bellamy was just beginning an infamous career that, over its span, resulted in at least fifty captured ships, and his greatest prizes still lay beyond the horizon.

Bellamy, Williams, and La Buse sailed together for some time and captured several fat prizes, despite being hunted by British warships looking to stamp out piracy at the command of Woodes Rogers, a former privateer who was now governor of the Bahamas. Eventually, La Buse's men decided to take their share of the plunder and head out on their own. They left on good terms with their English comrades but must not have been interested in Bellamy's master plan: to capture a truly massive ship and create his own man-of-war capable of withstanding, and possibly destroying, the British warships that hunted him and his brethren. Bellamy was tired of running; he wanted to be able to make a stand and fight. But to do so would require a vessel that was fast, strong, and maneuverable. He had heard of such a vessel . . . a Dutch slave ship newly built in London and named the *Whydah*. It sailed from Europe to Africa to the Caribbean and then back to Europe. If the stories were correct, she might just be the ship of Bellamy's dreams.

The pirates conferred among themselves and decided to return to the Windward Passage between Cuba and Hispaniola, where they would be most likely to encounter a large combat-capable ship. This move saw Bellamy and Williams returning to the very waters where they had begun their piratical adventure after the fruitless search for salvage off the coast of Florida. But now, a year and a half later, Bellamy was commanding nearly three times the men and firepower he had in the two periaguas. Bellamy and Williams had started out as common thieves, but as they attracted more and more sailors, slaves, and servants to their cause, month by month they had become the leaders of a nascent revolution. They desperately needed a proper flagship, worthy of the man whom all of the Caribbean had come to know as Captain "Black Sam" Bellamy.

Unbeknownst to the pirates, at that very moment the well-armed slave ship *Whydah* was in Port Royal, Jamaica, preparing to depart for London. The *Whydah* had everything a pirate could want. She was powerful, with eighteen large cannons and room for ten more. She was fairly maneuverable, with large sails and a shallow draft for a ship her size, and she was fast: a galley-built three-master capable of speeds up to thirteen knots. Best of all, the *Whydah* had an ample hold, designed to transport five hundred to seven hundred slaves; this would serve well to haul massive piles of cargo, loot, booty, or riches as required. The *Whydah* represented the most advanced technology of her age and could be extremely dangerous if she fell into the wrong hands. And the "wrong hands" were sailing to the Windward Passage to lie in wait for their time to pounce.

The *Whydah* weighed anchor during the last week of February 1717 under the command of a Captain Prince, who hoped to make a direct run to London after having been away from home for almost a year. His plan required him to sail the *Whydah* past eastern Cuba, Hispaniola, and most dangerously, the Bahamas, all of which were known pirate waters. But Prince was confident that the *Whydah* was fast and powerful enough to hold her own against a few pirate sloops.

When he was only a few days out, Prince saw that he was being followed. At first he concluded that the medium-size warship and the sloop-of-war tailing in his wake were British ships stationed in Jamaica, but it slowly became apparent that these were not Royal Navy vessels. They were pirate ships. Worse still, they were commanded by the notorious Black Sam Bellamy. The pirates were on an intercept course and were closing in, so the *Whydah*'s captain decided to make a run for it. The chase lasted three days. The pirates, through careful and clever seamanship, eventually closed in on the faster Dutch vessel after a pursuit that ranged over three hundred miles of open water.

Bellamy assessed that he, Williams, and their combined force could probably take the larger vessel in a fight, but the battle could cause extensive damage to all three ships—damage that might be difficult or

impossible to repair, especially at sea. So he decided to try to intimidate Captain Prince into surrendering. The pirates put on a wild display. Many of them wore fine clothing stolen from the wealthy captains
and passengers they had plundered: gentlemen's waistcoats, cuffs and
collars, elaborate hats of silk and felt, even wigs and plumes. On these
rough, wild-looking, barbarous men, this finery obviously represented
trophies captured in battle. Particularly terrifying to Captain Prince and
his crew of slavers were the twenty-five black men scattered among the
pirates, their unshackled hands brandishing weapons and a murderous
look in their eyes.

Prince surrendered after having fired only two shots. The pirates
swarmed over the *Whydah*, shouting and screaming triumphantly.
Black Sam Bellamy had acquired a ship worthy of the great Henry
Avery himself. The poor farm boy from England's West Country was
now a pirate prince in his own right.

The pirates set about refitting and arming their new flagship. They
transferred their treasure and cargo aboard and loaded as many cannons onto her as she could hold. They released Captain Prince and his
crewmen to make their way back to England in one of Bellamy's old,
worn-out ships. When Bellamy took command of the *Whydah*, he was
delighted to discover chests and strongboxes stuffed full of gold coins
hidden between her decks. The haul amounted to an estimated
60,000 to 70,000 pounds sterling (worth millions of dollars in today's
equivalent). This was the company's profit from the sale of a cargo of
African slaves hauled to the Caribbean. It had been bound for British
and Dutch investors but would now sail with the *Whydah* and her new
pirate masters.

The pirates had quickly become wealthy beyond their wildest
dreams, and they had one of the best ships on the ocean. Now they
wanted to test her capabilities. In early March, Bellamy gathered the
crew together to decide what to do with their "ship of force." Spring
was here, so they agreed to advance up the Eastern Seaboard of North
America, seizing ships as they passed in and out of the gates of the
Chesapeake and Delaware Bays and the harbors of Charleston and
New York. The plan was that Bellamy would take command of the
Whydah, while Williams would command the sloop *Marianne* as a
consort. If separated by bad weather or unforeseen events, the two
ships would rendezvous at Damariscove Island in Maine. Bellamy had

his sights set on eventually returning to Boston and reuniting with the lovely young lass he had left behind. For both pirate captains, it would be a triumphant homecoming. Williams would stop at Block Island, Rhode Island, and Bellamy would return to the Outer Cape to visit Mary Hallett.

They captured and plundered two more ships between the Bahamas and Florida on their way northward. They stayed well off-shore of the Carolinas, intending to make a beeline for the entrance to the Chesapeake Bay. Despite being more than a hundred miles out to sea, they crossed paths with a small merchant sloop out of Newport, Rhode Island. The sloop's master, a Captain Beer, was bound for Charleston and had probably opted for an outside passage in an effort to avoid the pirates said to be infesting the Florida Straits and Windward Passage. Instead, Beer found himself taken captive aboard the largest and most formidable pirate ship he or any of his fellow sailors had ever seen.

Beer spent only two hours aboard the *Whydah* while the pirates searched his vessel. He subsequently wrote about everything that had transpired, including a detailed account of his conversation with Sam Bellamy in which the pirate commodore expounded on the supposed political motivations behind his career. Both Williams and Bellamy were in favor of giving Beer his sloop, which was too small to be of any use to them, but their men, their egos inflated by their recent successes, refused. Bellamy ordered Beer brought before him so that he could give the unfortunate captain the bad news. In an apologetic voice, Bellamy said:

Damn my blood, I am sorry they wont let you have your sloop again, for I scorn to do anyone a mischief when it is not for my advantage. . . . Damn the sloop, we must sink her and she might have been use to you. . . . Damn ye, you are a sneaking puppy, and so are all those who will submit to be governed by laws which rich men have made for their own security, for the cowardly whelps have not the courage otherwise to defend what they get by their knavery. . . . But damn ye altogether! Damn them [as] a pack of crafty Rascals. And you [captains and seamen], who serve them, [as] a parcel of hen-hearted numbskulls! They vilify us, the scoundrels do, when there is only this difference [between us]: they rob the poor under the cover of law . . . and we plunder the rich under the cover of our own courage. . . . [Would] you not better make one of us, then [*sic*] sneak after the asses of those villains for employment?

Captain Beer took a few moments to consider his reply, and then said that his conscience would not allow him to "break through the laws of God and man." Bellamy continued:

You are a devilish conscient[ious] rascal damn ye. I am a free Prince, and I have as much authority to make war on the whole world as he who has a hundred ships at sea and an army of 100,000 men in the field. And <u>this</u> my conscience tells me. . . . There is no arguing with such sniveling puppies who allow superiors to kick them about [the] deck with pleasure, and [who] pin their faith upon a pimp of a Parson, a squab who neither practices nor believes what he [tells] the chuckle-headed fools he preaches to.

With that, Bellamy ordered Beer away. He ordered his crewmen to row the captain back over to the *Marianne*, so that Williams could leave him on Block Island when they arrived there. Once they finished plundering Beer's ship of its humble cargo of cider and foodstuffs, they set the sloop on fire and sailed away.

Bellamy and Williams made their way to the coast but got trapped in a thick fog that closed in too fast to allow their ships time to close ranks before both vessels were engulfed. The ships lost track of each other in the dark, and when morning came and the fog lifted to reveal the Virginia Capes, the *Marianne* was nowhere to be seen. Bellamy assured his crew that they would catch up to Williams and the rest of the crew at Block Island or, failing that, at Damariscove Island as planned. Meanwhile, they had riches to acquire.

Cruising off the coast of Virginia on the morning of April 9, 1717, Bellamy and his men spied and captured three merchant ships. All three surrendered with virtually no resistance; for the pirates, it was as easy as picking fruit off a tree. The *Whydah* was simply too big and powerful for a small merchant vessel to fight, and she was too fast to outrun. The pirates plundered all three ships, keeping one for a cargo ship because the hold of the *Whydah* was already groaning with plunder and cargo.

While Bellamy was taking his latest prizes, Paul Williams and his crew on the *Marianne* were just a few miles over the horizon near the Virginia Capes, searching for prey of their own. Williams no longer looked like the middle-aged son of a wealthy merchant. His white wig stood in stark contrast to his richly tanned skin. His motley crew, consisting of five Frenchmen, five Africans, an Indian, and nearly thirty Brits, looked as rough as the *Marianne* herself. One can only imagine what impression he thought he would make on his friends and family back in Rhode Island, but he was eager to return home. Without the firepower of the *Whydah* by his side, Williams had to choose his targets carefully and was having mixed success.

He captured several ships while hiding near the shallows off what is now Virginia Beach but was anxious to reunite with the *Whydah* and was keeping a sharp eye out for her along the coast. The crew and officers of the *Marianne* were also anxious to see their flagship, though their concern may have been less out of fear for their safety than for their separation from the treasure nestled in the *Whydah*'s hold. Williams knew that HMS *Shoreham* was protecting the Chesapeake, and after a few close calls, he decided to sail for Rhode Island, where he hoped the *Whydah* and his old friend Sam Bellamy would be waiting.

Williams arrived triumphantly at Block Island, where he sold their goods and cargo via his family connections with black marketers. The crew of the *Marianne* ate, drank, and reveled in their success. But there was no sign of the *Whydah*. Eventually, Williams released Captain Beer and sailed to Governors Island near the mouth of Long Island Sound. While cruising for prey entering New York Harbor, a fearsome storm started to rage, forcing him to shelter the *Marianne* behind the nearby Gardiners Island. This was going to be a terrible gale, and heaven help those who were far out at sea or farther north up the New England coast, where the storm was intensifying.

Meanwhile, after hunting the waters of the Virginia Capes for several weeks, attacking, capturing, and looting virtually every vessel that had come his way, Sam Bellamy decided the time had come to sail north. He made a stop at Block Island, but the *Marianne* had already left, so he continued up the coast and was nearing Cape Cod when he delayed slightly to capture two more merchant vessels. As he headed toward the cape, a heavy fog rolled in. Hidden by the blanket of fog, he captured a small merchant sloop out of Virginia bound for Boston. The captain of the vessel, a man named Ingols, knew these waters well, and Bellamy forced him to serve as pilot and guide the pirates and their captured vessels into Cape Cod.

About ten o'clock that night, the mighty storm hit. Driving rain, flashes of lightning, and gale-force winds drove the *Whydah* headlong toward the unseen, blackened coastline of the cape. In an effort to prevent his ship from crashing into the rocks, Bellamy tried to drop anchor, but the wind was simply too strong. The *Whydah* was a mighty vessel, but she was no match for the fury of nature, and the storm drove her helplessly forward until she ran aground on a sandbar. The resilient ship remained mired helplessly until the raging storm filled her sails, ripping away her masts, and tore the ship in half, rolling her severed body over to sink into the cold waters of the Atlantic.

As the storm raged on through the morning hours, the ebbing tide deposited more and more corpses on the shore. Amid the bloated, mangled bodies, only two men stirred. One was John Julian, a Mosquito Indian who had served with Bellamy aboard his periaguas. The other was Thomas Davis, a carpenter whom the pirates had pressed into service aboard the *Whydah*. Both of them were eventually captured and taken to Boston Prison. Black Sam Bellamy and at least 160 of his men perished in the sea that had brought them fame and fortune. At the time of the wreck, the *Whydah* was believed to have been carrying at least four and a half tons of gold, silver, and jewels, as well as other valuable cargo—truly an incredible fortune in any century.

Paul Williams, unaware of the fate of the *Whydah*, stuck to the original plan and made his way up the coast after the storm abated. They picked up several prizes en route but delayed passage as they made their way toward Maine. They waited at the rendezvous point for weeks, making necessary repairs to the dilapidated *Marianne*. Finally, fearing that his friend may have run into problems, Williams and his men decided to make their way back south. They would prey on whatever victims crossed their path and keep a sharp eye out for Bellamy until they eventually reached Nassau in the Bahamas.

While sailing south past Cape Cod, Williams captured a small fishing vessel. From its crew, he learned of the fate of the *Whydah*. The flagship, the treasure, and his dear friend all were gone, destroyed by the sea. A storm had once prompted the two men to leave New England to go hunting for treasure in the Florida Keys, and now a second storm had taken back all the stolen treasure on the verge of their triumphant return home. Nothing more is known of Paul Williams, the *Marianne*, or the crewmen who had once sailed proudly with the self-proclaimed pirate prince Samuel Bellamy.

As for the *Whydah*, although much of her treasure was looted by locals shortly after she sank, the actual wreck site remained lost until she was rediscovered in 1984 by underwater explorer Barry Clifford. Since then, the shipwreck has been the site of extensive underwater archaeology. Divers have retrieved more than two hundred thousand individual pieces, including the ship's bell, whose inscription, THE WHYDAH GALLY 1716, positively identified the wreck. It is the only pirate shipwreck site to date whose identification has been established beyond a shadow of a doubt.

Work on the site by Clifford's dive team continues on an annual basis. Selected artifacts from the wreck are displayed at Expedition Whydah Sea-Lab and Learning Center (The Whydah Pirate Museum) in Provincetown, Massachusetts. A collection of the artifacts has also been on a tour across the United States under the sponsorship of the National Geographic Society.

Edward "Blackbeard" Teach

Come all you jolly sailors
You all so stout and brave;
Come hearken and I'll tell you
What happen'd on the wave.
Oh! 'tis of that bloody Blackbeard
I'm going now for to tell;
And as how by gallant Maynard
He soon was sent to hell.
—Benjamin Franklin (attributed)

Of all of the real, historical pirates who ever lived to terrorize the world's shipping lanes, Blackbeard is certainly the most infamous. His life and legend have made him the subject of hundreds of books, films, and stories. There are so many stories about Blackbeard that it has become nearly impossible to separate fact from pure fancy. If we believed everything we read, we would have to accept that Blackbeard was everywhere at once, personally killed hundreds if not thousands of people, and buried untold amounts of treasure on nearly every beach in the world. So where among the stories and legends do we find the real Blackbeard, and what connection did he actually have with Virginia?

Blackbeard's origins are murky. Some said his real name was Teach, Tash, Tatch, Tack, Tache, or Thatch. A few sources claim that he was born Edward Drummond in Bristol, England; others say he hailed from Accomack County, Virginia. Whatever name he acquired at birth, and wherever that birth took place, it was under the name Blackbeard that he gained notoriety as one of history's most wanted men. It was a name that caused honest seamen to quake and that parents used to threaten children before bedtime.

The details of Teach's early life are scarce. His earliest appearance in the historical record shows him serving as a privateer off Jamaica during the War of the Spanish Succession. When the war came to an end in 1714, Teach, like many other sailors, privateers, mariners, and compatriots, found themselves without work or purpose. Knowing nothing beyond attacking ships and looting, Teach turned his hand to piracy. The ensuing era of peace created a restlessness of spirit that led him to sign on as a crew member with the pirate captain Benjamin Hornigold, whose base of operations was New Providence in the Bahamas. Teach quickly distinguished himself with his strength, courage, and devil-may-care attitude.

He rose quickly under Hornigold and by 1716 had been placed in command of a sloop taken in combat. The following year, Hornigold, in command of the brigantine *Ranger*, with Teach commanding his consort sloop, set out to cruise off the mainland of America. En route, the two pirate ships easily took and plundered a sloop from Havana laden with 120 barrels of flour, another from Bermuda with a cargo of wine, and a ship bound from Madeira for Charleston, South Carolina, with a tantalizingly vague cargo "of great value."

Arriving off the Virginia capes late in the summer of 1717, the two pirates found it necessary to clean the barnacle-encrusted hulls of their ships. They selected an isolated backwater of the eastern shore of Virginia, where they careened the vessels and made ready to return to sea. On September 29, they encountered, attacked, and captured the Virginia sloop *Betty* near Cape Charles. They plundered and scuttled the *Betty*, which carried a cargo of Madeira wine and other goods and merchandise.

Hornigold and Teach then set their sights and their rudders northward. On October 22, in Delaware Bay, they seized and plundered the sloop *Robert* of Philadelphia and the merchant ship *Good Intent* out of Dublin, both bound for the port of Philadelphia and heavily laden with cargo and merchandise.

After preying successfully for several months along the Virginia coast and the entrance to the Chesapeake Bay, the pirates decided to return to the West Indies, their ships loaded with plunder. In December, they spotted a large Dutch-built French slaver bound for Martinique off the coast of St. Vincent in the Bahamas. After a few broadsides and a brief exchange of fire, the vessel, named the *Concord*, surrendered. She proved to be an extremely rich prize. The *Concord* was carrying not only a valuable cargo of slaves bound for Martinique, but also a large quantity of gold dust, gold and silver coins, plate, and jewels. She was a large and powerful ship, though lightly crewed considering her mission as a slave transport. But she withstood the cannon fire well and still sailed easily. Teach wanted her for himself, so he requested the ship from Hornigold, who, having grown both tired and wealthy from his sea roving, had begun to contemplate retirement from piracy. Hornigold consented, and Teach quickly had the *Concord* armed with forty guns, manned by a crew of nearly three hundred men, and renamed the *Queen Anne's Revenge*.

Now that Teach was in command of his own ship, he and Hornigold parted ways. Hornigold accepted the king's pardon and lived an honest life of obscene luxury on his ill-gotten fortune. Teach, meanwhile, sought to reinvent himself by cultivating a fearsome reputation . . . as Blackbeard. He intentionally developed this evil renown as an aid in encouraging his victims to promptly surrender with minimal resistance. His tall frame and powerful physique contributed to his fearful appearance, made all the more menacing by a long, coal-black beard, which, before action, he plaited into small pigtails tied with colored ribbons. Into these he braided slow-burning fuses, pieces of cordite ordinarily used to touch off cannons. The wisps of smoke curling out from beneath his cocked hat and around his face greatly increased his devilish look. Across his chest he wore a bandolier, in which he usually carried six primed, cocked, ready-to-fire pistols, and in his belt were an assortment of daggers and a cutlass..

A firm believer in the importance of first impressions, he ordinarily dressed completely in black to create an appearance as horrifying as his deeds. Blackbeard in battle array was an awesome sight, and sailors of the day feared him as much as the devil himself, to whom many believed him a close relative. This fearsome demeanor, combined with his reputation for bloodthirsty ruthlessness, resulted in the instant surrender of many of his victims.

During this period, a successful hunt by the pirates in the sea lanes between the Bahamas and South Carolina led the *Queen Anne's Revenge* to take at least twelve ships, and predictably, some of the captured sailors signed on with Blackbeard's crew. Blackbeard had by now amassed a considerable fortune but was having difficulty controlling and supplying his massive three-hundred-man crew. Managing a crew of quarrelsome cutthroats on the open sea was a tricky business, even for men who lived in constant terror of a captain as feared as Blackbeard. In his journal, which was discovered aboard his ship after his death, lay a clue to his management style: "Such a day, rum all out!— Our company somewhat sober:—A damn'd confusion amongst us!— Rogues a-plotting:—Great talk of separation—so I looked sharp for a prize: Such a day took one, with a great deal of liquor on board, so kept the company hot, damned hot; then all things went well again." Blackbeard's psychopathic personality craved near-constant excitement liberally seasoned with cruelty, danger, and terror, and he felt the occasional barbarous display was a necessary component of maintaining discipline and discouraging mutiny. During one lower-deck meeting with his men, he extinguished the lantern and fired his pistol randomly under the table, crippling a crewman. Another time, he closeted himself in the hold with several crewmen and directed that pots of sulfur—then called brimstone and believed to fuel the fires of hell—be lit. Soon, clouds of choking acrid fumes forced the others to flee, and a grinning Blackbeard was the last to walk through the door.

But even Blackbeard could keep his crew under control for only so long, and he decided it was time to sell off the mountain of plunder and riches filling the hold of the *Queen Anne's Revenge*. With a change of plan in mind, Blackbeard sailed for North Carolina's Pamlico Sound as the commodore of a flotilla of four ships. The shallow sounds were protected by the Outer Banks and provided a number of hiding places large enough to conceal a pirate fleet. One retreat Blackbeard occasionally used was up the Chowan River near Holiday's Island, but his favorite refuge was Ocracoke Island, where a house known as Blackbeard's Castle once stood in the village. An inlet not far from the present town of Ocracoke is known today as Teach's Hole, and tradition has it that he careened his ships here for repair.

Following Hornigold's example, he appeared before Governor Charles Eden of North Carolina with twenty of his men and politely received the king's pardon. The arrival in the little town of the blackest and most infamous outlaw and pirate on the Atlantic coast must have been as traumatic to the governor as it was a cause for great excitement to the general populace. Undoubtedly intimidated from their first meeting, Governor Eden drew up pardons for all of the cutthroats. Blackbeard, with his band of brigands and a well-armed vessel to back him up, immediately "cultivated a very good understanding" with the intimidated governor and decided to settle in town—directly across the street from the governor's home. A contemporary account describes chests of pirate loot being carried to Governor Eden's house and makes the sly observation that "Governors are but Men."

Blackbeard quickly became something of a local celebrity, courted by planters who relished an association with the famous outlaw, and lived the life of a wealthy gentleman. He even had Governor Eden marry him to a sixteen-year-old bride who, unbeknownst to her, was actually his fourteenth wife. Twelve of the fourteen were still living, and he had not been divorced from any of them. The poor girl's marriage to the infamous pirate would prove less than pleasant. According to at least one report, Blackbeard's appetites were as bestial as his reputation suggests. As the story goes, on one occasion, while his ship lay at anchor in Ocracoke inlet, he was ashore with his wife, with whom he had spent the night. For some unknown reason, possibly to amuse himself or merely to show the young girl her place in the course of things, he invited five or six of his more brutish companions to come ashore and forced his wife to prostitute herself to each of them, one after another, while the men laughed and drank and watched. Although this incident may or may not be true, it became a part of Blackbeard's fearsome legend and reputation that intimidated his foes so very well.

An extended period of merrymaking and dissipation followed Blackbeard's conversion to the honest life. During this time, the pirate, though a swaggering braggart, won over most of the neighboring planters through gifts of rum and sugar, as well as lavish entertainment in his home. His crew had also received the king's pardon, and a number of them quickly became bored and restless. It came as no surprise that some soon slipped away to resume their former trade.

Some struck out for New York and Philadelphia, while others, such as Teach's quartermaster, William Howard, went to Virginia. Those who remained became increasingly boisterous, rowdy, and troublesome to the honest colonists of North Carolina.

It became all too clear to Governor Eden, who lacked any suitable defense against this murderous gang of cutthroats, that the pirates had sought pardon not "from any reformation of manners, but only to wait a more favorable opportunity to play the game again." Blackbeard, for his part, acted as if he owned the place . . . which may not have been far from the truth. But he played rough and began to lord his invincibility over the town. When his men became rowdy and the locals asked him to keep them under control, he threatened the town with fire and sword if any injury occurred to him or his companions. On one occasion, suspecting that a plan was afoot to capture him, he drew up his sloop against the town and went ashore to the governor's house, armed to the teeth, leaving orders with his gunners that if he should not return within an hour, they were to "batter the house about their ears," even if he were still inside.

After a while, however, Blackbeard, like many of his crewmen before him, began to grow bored with the pleasures of terrifying one small town in North Carolina. Certainly he had wealth and fame and luxury, but where was the adventure? Where was the excitement? Where was the danger? He had tired of this game. Eventually, perhaps inevitably, the call of the open sea became irresistible, and Blackbeard returned to piracy.

He set sail for Philadelphia, where he picked up additional crewmen and sold off some of his remaining contraband. He did not, however, remain there for long, because a warrant for his arrest had been issued by William Keith, governor of Pennsylvania, and two sloops were already being outfitted to track him down. Blackbeard decided not to wait around to see if Pennsylvania would honor the terms of his pardon from North Carolina, so he concluded his business, set sail, and made his way south.

Tradition in the James River region maintains that Blackbeard eluded British naval vessels by disappearing up Pagan Creek in the neighborhood of Smithfield, Virginia. Blackbeard's Hill still dominates Lynnhaven Bay near Cape Henry. From its summit, pirate sentinels could scan the Chesapeake Bay entrance through the Virginia Capes.

Ultimately, Edward Teach pushed the tolerance and endurance of everyone he encountered beyond their limits by his insolence, insults, and brutal thefts. Because most of Virginia's cargoes traveled through the Chesapeake Bay, trade in the colony came to a standstill whenever pirates patrolled sea lanes, and threatened vessels feared to leave the safety of their ports. During one six-week period, not a single ship dared leave or enter Virginia's harbors.

Winter approached and Blackbeard sailed south to range across the waters of the Caribbean until the spring of 1718, when he came up with a bold new plan. After wintering in the Caribbean, Blackbeard sailed north to Charleston, South Carolina. Working in tandem with three other sloops he had captured, the *Queen Anne's Revenge* audaciously blockaded the city's harbor, attacking any ship that attempted to leave or enter. The locals were ill equipped to repel the piratical blockade, so they sent out emissaries to argue for mercy, pleading that their city could not survive if all shipping were cut off. In true "Blackbeard" style, Teach took the emissaries prisoner and held them for ransom. He sent ashore a landing party with instructions to bring back costly medical supplies—namely, medicinal mercury, then believed to cure syphilis—to treat diseases that plagued his crew. Teach promised to release the prisoners in exchange for the supplies, which, in due course, he did.

The governor of South Carolina described the outlandish incident in a report to his superiors in London:

[The pirates] appeared in sight of the town, took our pilotboat and afterwards 8 or 9 sailed with several of the best inhabitants of this place on board and then sent me word if I did not immediately send them a chest of medicines they would put every prisoner to death, which for their sakes being complied with after plundering them of all they had were sent ashore almost naked.

Having thoroughly terrified Charleston, Teach next sailed up the coast to New Jersey's Little Egg Harbor, making one of the numerous small islands located behind Brigantine Island his temporary hideout and headquarters. While Blackbeard was whiling away his time by carousing along the New Jersey coast, British ships and troops mounted a massive, well-targeted search for the elusive rogue.

For several months, Blackbeard passed the time in the sounds off the North Carolina coast. The *Queen Anne's Revenge* would sometimes lie at anchor in various coves and at other times sail from one inlet to another, trading with whatever sloops Blackbeard might encounter if he was in a bartering mood, or simply taking what he wanted if he was not. Occasionally he ventured ashore to visit the planters, where he reveled for days on end, presenting stolen gifts to his hosts and taking liberties with their wives and daughters, which no one dared contest. Even from a distance, he continued to bully Governor Eden, who had little choice but to acquiesce and turn a blind eye to Blackbeard's exploits and a deaf ear to the colonists' complaints.

As time passed, the malingering presence of Blackbeard and his crewmen became an unbearable burden to the inhabitants of the Carolina coast. It was obvious that any plea to the governor of North Carolina would be in vain, so in desperation, they sought assistance elsewhere. They needed a real pirate fighter—someone with the resolve, dedication, incorruptibility, and force of arms to bring the devil to heel. The man they found who embodied all of these traits was Alexander Spotswood, governor of Virginia.

All through the summer of 1718, Williamsburg, Virginia, was rife with unrest. Governor Spotswood was mired in a heated quarrel with influential members of the local gentry. Eight members of the Virginia Colonial Council had declined to attend his elegant annual entertainment in honor of the king's birthday in May of that year. Instead, as the governor observed, they "got together all the turbulent and disaffected Burgesses, had an entertainment of their own in the Burgesses House and invited the mobb [sic] to a bonfire where they were plentifully supplied with liquors."

Stung by the largely unmerited volley of acrimonious accusations and resulting recriminations leveled at him by well-connected colonial gentlemen, Spotswood recognized an opportunity to champion a popular cause that would help restore his personal standing when merchants from North Carolina pleaded with him to help rid the coast of their state as well as Virginia of the dreaded Blackbeard. Many of them attested to collusion between their own governor, Charles Eden, and the pirates. While Spotswood mulled the political advantages of authorizing a search for Blackbeard, the pirate's quartermaster, William Howard, was captured in Virginia and charged with serving under "one Edward Tach and other Wickid and desolute Persons." To push Spotswood further toward a decision, it was learned that the sea rovers were planning to fortify Ocracoke Island as a permanent stronghold. Time was of the essence in order to dispatch an expedition before Okracoke became impregnable. If left unchecked, the pirates might well engulf the entirety of Virginia mercantile shipping and the very shores of the Chesapeake itself.

With both North Carolina and Virginia suffering from a bad case of Blackbeard fever, their population now attributed every pirate act committed along the shoreline, and every strange sail sighted, to Teach; his villainous reputation had grown far larger than the man himself. Deciding that he would do what the governor of North Carolina would not, Spotswood resolved to put an end to the black-hearted pirate and his evil minions. He demanded that his government vote in favor of "speedy and Effectual Measures for breaking up that Knott of Robbers."

Without consulting his government, Spotswood quietly sent for pilots from North Carolina who were familiar with the shoals and inlets of that colony. He issued a proclamation offering rewards for the capture—dead or alive—of Teach and his shipmates, and he personally provided the funds to hire two sloops and put the Carolinian pilots aboard at his own expense. Going one bold step further, Spotswood decided to invade North Carolina and destroy this seething nest of hornets before it grew and spread to the shores of his own colony.

Spotswood also enlisted the help of British naval officers in organizing an expedition to capture the infamous pirate, even though the Carolina shoreline, where Blackbeard sheltered his ship, was well beyond his jurisdiction. But the governor was well aware that even the Royal Navy might be reluctant to risk lives against the likes of Blackbeard, who had already fought a Royal Navy frigate to a draw. There was even the chance that a few of those sent to capture him might switch sides unless there was an ample incentive not to do so. Consequently, the governor promised a bonus from the Virginia Assembly over and above the reward they would receive under the king's proclamation. On November 14, an "Act to Encourage the Apprehending and Destroying of Pyrates" was passed, and a 100-pound bounty was offered for the death or capture of Blackbeard.

On November 17, 1718, the governor's two sloops, commanded by an experienced British naval officer named Lieutenant Robert

Maynard, slipped stealthily out of the Chesapeake Bay into the Atlantic on their way to Ocracoke Island. Maynard reached the appointed area on the evening of November 21. Because the pirate ships were anchored in shallow waters that were difficult to navigate, he approached the enemy in two launches too small to carry cannons. This meant his crew would be forced to take on the most dangerous pirate in the world in hand-to-hand combat with cutlass and pistols. Being as cautious as possible, Maynard waited until morning to attack.

As morning broke across the water, Maynard's ships—the *Jane* and the *Ranger*—slipped toward Ocracoke Island. Spotting the approaching ships, the pirates sounded the alarm and hoisted anchor. Maynard's vessels chased the pirate ships using oars, since there was too little wind to fill even their small sails. While attempting to navigate the shallow, unfamiliar waters strewn with sandbars, Maynard's ship ran aground.

With the pirate ship becalmed and Maynard's sloop grounded, a shouting match between Lieutenant Maynard and Captain Teach now ensued. In his *General History of the Pirates*, Captain Charles Johnson described the exchange as follows:

> Black-Beard hail'd him in this rude Manner: "Damn you for Villains, who are you? and from whence come you?" The Lieutenant make him Answer, "You may see by our Colours [the flags that identified a ship] we are no Pyrates." Black-beard bid him send his Boat on Board, that he might see who he was but Mr. Maynard reply'd thus; "I cannot spare my Boat, but I will come aboard of you as soon as I can, with my Sloop." Upon this Black-beard took a Glass of Liquor, & drank to him with these Words: "Damnation seize my Soul if I give you Quarter [mercy], or take any from you." In Answer to which, Mr. Maynard told him, that he expected no Quarters from him, nor should he give him any.

Eventually Maynard's crew managed to free their vessels. As they rowed steadily toward Blackbeard's ship, Teach unleashed a broadside volley, killing several of Maynard's men and wounding others. Reeling from the assault but seeing an opportunity for subterfuge, Maynard ordered the remainder of his crewmen to conceal themselves below deck.

When the smoke cleared, Teach reasonably assumed that the broadside attack had killed most of Maynard's men. The British launches came within range of Blackbeard's ship, and Teach and some of his men climbed aboard the *Jane*. As soon as the pirates boarded their ship, Maynard's crew leaped out from their hiding places and engaged the brigands in a ferocious hand-to-hand battle on deck. According to Captain Johnson's account, Blackbeard "stood his ground and fought with great fury till he received five and twenty wounds." Of Teach's twenty-five wounds, the last was fatal—the legend had fallen.

The year after Blackbeard's death, the *Boston News Letter* published a detailed account of the pirate's last battle:

Maynard and Teach themselves began the fight with their swords, Maynard making a thrust, the point of his sword went against Teach's cartridge box, and bended it to the hilt. Teach broke the guard of it, and wounded Maynard's fingers but did not disable him, whereupon he [Maynard] jumped back and threw away his sword and fired his pistol which wounded Teach. Demelt [one of Maynard's sailors] struck in between them with his sword and cut Teach's face pretty much; in the interim both companies engaged in Maynard's sloop, one of Maynard's men . . . engaged Teach with his broad sword, who gave Teach a cut on the neck, Teach saying well done lad; [the man] replied If it be not well done, I'll do it better. With that he gave him a second stroke, which cut off his head, laying it flat on his shoulder.

The Battle of Ocracoke Inlet, as it came to be known, though it lasted only minutes, was one of the bloodiest naval actions on record, for its size and the number of men involved. Though accounts differ, casualties were extremely high on both sides. As many as twenty-nine of Maynard's sixty-four men were killed and wounded, while Blackbeard and eight of the fourteen crewmen that had boarded Maynard's ship were killed and the rest wounded.

Maynard's crew threw Teach's headless corpse overboard. According to legend, his headless body swam around the ship before disappearing into its murky grave. They hung the bearded head of the infamous pirate from the bowsprit of Maynard's boat as a warning to other sea robbers. The head also offered concrete proof of Teach's death, allowing Maynard to collect the bounty Governor Spotswood had placed on the pirate's head. "Here," remarked a contemporary, "was an end to that courageous brute, who might have passed in the world for a hero had he been employed in a good cause."

Stopping first at Bath, North Carolina, Maynard discovered much of the pirates' booty in the barn of Tobias Knight, Governor Eden's secretary. With the recovered goods on board and Blackbeard's skull swinging from the bowsprit, the expedition returned to Virginia.

Williamsburg's first mayor, John Holloway, characterized by Spotswood as "a constant patron and advocate of pirates," defended Blackbeard's onetime quartermaster, William Howard, in court while the pirate was incarcerated in the town. Nine of Blackbeard's crew survived to be captured and, with six others seized in Bath, were brought to Virginia's colonial capital for trial, probably held in the general courtroom on the first floor of the capitol building. March 1719 saw thirteen pirates meet their end on the gallows along Williamsburg's present Capitol Landing Road.

During the seventeenth and eighteenth centuries, the bodies of executed pirates often were hanged in chains near harbor entrances and left for years as a warning to would-be pirates. It is recorded that Spotswood required this action to be taken, and four "profligate wretches" were hanged in pairs at Tindall's Point on the York and Urbanna on the Rappahannock. Blackbeard's skull hung for many years from a pole at the confluence of the Hampton and James Rivers. The site is still known as Blackbeard's Point. It was a loud and blatant warning to all who might have thought to undertake a life of piracy, meant to convey this message: "So you want to be a pirate, eh? Best do it elsewhere, matey. Look what we did to the legendary Blackbeard! Think you stand a chance? Don't mess with Virginia, you dogs!"

According to reputable sources, the old pirate's skull was later taken down and fashioned into a silver-mounted drinking cup. Antiquarian and publisher John F. Watson stated that Blackbeard's "skull was made into the bottom part of a very large punch bowl, called the infant, which was long used as a drinking vessel at the Raleigh Tavern in Williamsburg. It was enlarged with silver, or silver plated; and I have seen those whose forefathers have spoken of their drinking punch from it, with a silver ladle appurtenant to that bowl."

The legend of Blackbeard proliferated following the end of what has been termed the Golden Age of Piracy. A youthful Ben Franklin, then a printer's apprentice in Boston, wrote what he called "a sailor's song on the taking of Teach." A series of theatrical dramas ensued, and for a time, pirates and rumors of pirates continued to haunt the southern coast. Today Blackbeard's memory is kept alive in Williamsburg through interpretive programs at the capitol and gaol (jail).

The bloody battle with Blackbeard brought the Chesapeake a temporary respite from piracy. Yet the piratical plague was still a very real and menacing threat to the Tidewater region and, indeed, the entire Eastern Seaboard. But rather than ushering in a lasting peace, the defeat of the prime predator of the Atlantic coast cleared the way for others to follow in his wake. Less than a year after the Battle of Ocracoke Inlet, more than seventy different pirate crews were known to be plundering shipping off the North American coast. The plague of piracy was far from cured.

Major
Stede Bonnet

At the end of August 1717, a strange vessel entered Nassau harbor in the Bahamas. Her sails and rigging were in tatters, her decks scarred with the telltale wounds and debris of a prolonged battle. She was a sloop-of-war flying a black flag, but nobody in Nassau had ever seen her before. When her captain appeared on deck, a plump, well-groomed gentleman wearing a fine dressing gown and swaddled in bandages, onlookers were stunned. He looked for all the world as if he'd hardly spent a single day of his life at sea. None of the people who witnessed this genteel landlubber hobbling across the deck could have imagined that he was destined to become a leading accomplice of the notorious Blackbeard.

Stede Bonnet, the man in the dressing gown, was the most unlikely of pirates. He had been born on Barbados twenty-nine years earlier, in 1688, to an affluent family of sugar plantation owners. The English had settled Barbados in the late 1620s, at least a generation earlier than Jamaica or the Bahamas, and Stede's great-grandfather, Thomas, had been among the earliest pioneers. Over the next nine decades, the Bonnet family had cleared hundreds of acres of jungle to the southeast of the colony's capital, Bridgetown, planting it first with tobacco and then, more successfully, with sugarcane. Like other successful planters, they had purchased African slaves to tend the crops and the sweltering tubs of cane syrup in the sugarhouses.

Stede's early years were spent on the sprawling plantation, where his life was one of privilege, wealth, and position. But it was not entirely without tragedy. In 1694, when he was only six years old, his father passed away, and his mother appears to have died shortly thereafter.

The plantation was placed in the care of lawyers and guardians until such time as young master Bonnet came of age. He was now a lonely orphan child attended by three servants and ninety-four slaves while he was groomed to take his place among the Barbadian aristocracy. He received a liberal education, served as a major in the colony's militia, and courted the daughter of another rich plantation owner, William Allamby. In 1709, at age twenty-one, Bonnet married young Mary Allamby. They set up house and Bonnet was "generally esteemed and honoured." Then everything started to go horribly wrong.

Their first child died in early childhood, and her death had a lasting impact on Stede Bonnet. Three more children followed—Edward, Stede Jr., and Mary—yet Bonnet's spirit remained crushed. He fell into a deep depression, and seems to have suffered intermittent bouts of insanity. His friends and neighbors believed that he suffered from "a disorder in his Mind, which had been but too visible in him [for] some time," supposedly caused "by some discomforts he found in a married state."

By the end of 1716, Stede had reached the breaking point. While his fellow planters were in an uproar over the seizures and thefts carried out by the notorious pirates Black Sam Bellamy and Paul Williams (see earlier chapter), who were causing irreparable damage to the trade of the nearby Leeward Islands, Bonnet was enthralled by the devastation. Though he was a landsman through and through, and entirely ignorant of the arts of seamanship and navigation, he decided to build a warship of his very own. He contracted a local shipbuilder to construct a sixty-ton sloop-of-war capable of carrying up to a dozen cannons and seventy to eighty crewmen. He probably told the authorities that he intended to use the ship as a privateer, claiming he would go to Antigua or Jamaica, where he expected to be granted a commission to hunt down the pirates plaguing Caribbean shipping. But it is far more likely that he intended to become a pirate in his own right.

When the sloop was completed, Bonnet christened her the *Revenge* and set about hiring a crew. Betraying his ignorance of both privateer and pirate custom alike, he paid the men a cash salary instead of shares. He also would have needed to pay his officers extremely well, as he had to rely entirely on their expertise to operate, maintain, and repair his ship. While the officers began ordering the appropriate arms, stores, and provisions, Bonnet concentrated on the matter he believed most important to successful buccaneering: equipping his luxurious cabin with an extensive library.

When everything was ready, the *Revenge* slipped out of the harbor under the cover of darkness. Bonnet was leaving his wife behind with his infant daughter and three- and four-year-old sons and would never see any of them again. Once the ship moved safely into the open ocean, Major Bonnet assembled the men and loudly proclaimed from the quarterdeck that he was a pirate. This vainglorious act was probably unnecessary, for the seventy sailors on board were all desperate cutthroats of various nationalities, and they all knew perfectly well what was expected of them once they reached the sea lanes. But if Bonnet had not publicly declared himself a pirate, it is possible that he might not have been able to convince himself that he really was one. He ran a black flag up the mast, buckled on an ornate cutlass, and stood proudly on the quarterdeck: Stede Bonnet, pirate.

Knowing he would probably be recognized in the Leeward Islands, Bonnet ordered his officers to take the *Revenge* straight toward the colonial American mainland. Presumably no one would recognize Bonnet nineteen hundred miles from home, but on the way, he told the crew to refer to him as Captain Edwards, just in case. After leaving Barbados, Bonnet headed for the Virginia Capes, where he attacked and despoiled the *Anne of Glasgow*; the *Endeavor*, out of Bristol; the *Young*, from Leeds; and the *Turbes*, from Barbados, all of which he burned rather than risk the chance of reports of his activities returning to his home. From the capes, the *Revenge* sailed for New England, and off Block Island, Rhode Island, she captured a sloop bound for the West Indies. Bonnet then put in to Peconic Bay at the east end of Long Island and sent a small boat to Gardiners Island, where the pirates bought and paid for fresh provisions. Turning south, the *Revenge* spent time lurking in the waters beyond the bar outside the port of Charleston, South Carolina.

By this time, Bonnet had amply demonstrated to the crew his complete lack of seamanship, and although he had officers directing all the nautical operations, the mass of the crew had developed a seething contempt for their landlubber captain. They grumbled and growled, and many of the men would have been glad to throw Bonnet overboard and take the ship into their own hands. But when the slightest symptoms of mutiny began to appear, the pirates found that although their captain may have been an atrocious sailor, he was a very determined, slightly insane, and relentless taskmaster. Bonnet knew that the captain of a pirate ship ought to be the most severe and rigid man on board, so at the slightest sign of insubordination, he had his grumbling men put in chains or flogged. While the punishment was being carried out, Bonnet strutted around the deck with loaded pistols, threatening to kill any man who dared disobey him. Recognizing that although their captain was no sailor, he was a first-class tyrant, the rebellious crew kept their grumbling to themselves and worked his ship.

With the crew suitably intimidated, Bonnet sailed south, directing the *Revenge* toward Nassau in the Bahamas, the infamous home to an extensive pirate enclave. Although it is impossible to know for certain, it is likely that Bonnet set his sights on Nassau because he was in search of recognition, not as a Barbadian plantation owner, but as a dangerous, feared, and successful pirate captain who had already captured several wealthy prizes.

Somewhere near Cuba, however, the *Revenge* encountered a situation that nearly cost Major Bonnet his life. Any savvy pirate knew far better than to engage a ship that was more powerful than his own and could easily tell a lumbering merchant ship from a deadly man-of-war. Stede Bonnet, however, did not possess the ability to differentiate, and once he had set his sights on a prize, there was simply no reasoning with him. Through hubris, weakness, or gross incompetence, he allowed the *Revenge* to engage in a full-fledged battle with a Spanish warship. By the time his crew managed to retreat, the decks of the *Revenge* were awash with blood, more than half of his crew had been either killed or severely wounded, and Bonnet had suffered life-threatening injuries. The *Revenge* escaped, probably because she was faster and more agile than the Spanish man-of-war, suggesting that Bonnet could have avoided the encounter altogether.

As Bonnet lay bandaged and recuperating in his luxurious cabin, seeking solace from his agonizing pain in his extensive library, the surviving crewmen set a course for the ultimate sanctuary—New Providence Island and the pirate enclave at Nassau. Bonnet's landing there was much as we described it in the opening paragraph of our story. The pirate brethren of Nassau listened attentively and amusedly to Bonnet's story, and then to the reports of his men. In the private backroom discussions that followed, the pirates resolved to grant the eccentric planter refuge, at least until he recovered from his wounds, but they also cast covetous glances toward his fine, custom-built ship.

Among the infamous pirate captains who happened to be in Nassau during this encounter was the legendary Captain Benjamin Hornigold. It was Hornigold's opinion that his quartermaster, Edward Teach (later to become known as Blackbeard), could do big things with a fine ship of his own. If Teach were placed in charge of Bonnet's ship, which was vastly superior to the small sloop he had been commanding, the *Revenge* could be a valuable asset in supporting Hornigold's sea roving. Bonnet, who was barely able to leave his bed, would continue to occupy the captain's cabin, but Teach would command the ship. The offer was presented to Bonnet, and being in no position to argue, he accepted the deal.

Teach transferred many of his men and two cannons to the *Revenge* and commenced repairs on the new but damaged sloop-of-war. Within a few weeks, the *Revenge* had been repaired, equipped with twelve additional guns and 150 men, and was ready to depart. Hornigold had business to attend to, but first he made arrangements to meet up with Teach and the *Revenge* off the coast of Virginia in a few weeks' time.

Several weeks later, the *Revenge* was spotted a thousand miles to the north, patrolling the entrance to Delaware Bay, through which all of the merchant ships coming into or out of Philadelphia passed. During the trip from Nassau, all of Teach's doubts about Major Stede Bonnet were more than confirmed. While Bonnet languished in his cabin with his books, the crew of the *Revenge* told stories that made it clear that their gentleman captain, even when in fine health, was entirely unfit for command. On those occasions when Bonnet managed to venture out on deck in search of sea breezes and fresh air, he wore an elegant morning gown and carried whatever book he was currently reading. He may not have been an accomplished sailor like Teach, but his frail, elegant appearance underlined the fact that he was both wealthy and educated. His mental state was, however, similarly fragile, and Teach suspected it would take little effort to wrest permanent command of the *Revenge* from his tenuous grasp. Teach was pleasant to Bonnet, encouraging him to rest in his cabin, easy in the assurance that the ship was in good hands.

The *Revenge* did manage to capture one prize during this interlude: the forty-ton sloop *Betty* of Virginia, loaded with Madeira wine and other merchandise. On September 29, 1717, as they bore down on her at the Virginia Capes, Teach donned his terrifying new battle attire. He wore a silk sling over his shoulders, with "three brace of pistols, hanging in holsters like bandoliers" attached. Under his hat, he tied lit fuses, allowing some of them to dangle beside his face, surrounding his head in a halo of smoke and fire and causing his eyes to become red and watery. He presented such a fearsome aspect, a contemporary biographer reported, "his eyes naturally looking fierce and wild," that he "made altogether such a figure that imagination cannot form an idea of a fury from Hell to look more frightful." The crew of the *Betty* took one look at this fearsome devil, surrounded by an army of wild men armed with muskets, pistols, cutlasses, pikes, and grenades, and wisely chose to surrender their cargo with hardly a shot fired. Teach was now known as Blackbeard, and he was firmly in command of Bonnet's fine ship.

In an effort to prevent the *Betty* from alerting all of Virginia and Maryland to the presence of the pirates, Blackbeard ordered all the captives to be brought aboard the *Revenge*. William Howard, Blackbeard's quartermaster, drilled holes in the *Betty*'s hull and then rowed back to the *Revenge* as the prize slowly sank beneath the waves off the Virginia Capes. The swaggering pirates boasted to their captives that they were awaiting their consort, "a ship of forty guns," and that once she arrived, they intended to sail up the Delaware and lay siege to Philadelphia itself. Others bragged that they planned to sail down to Virginia to capture "a good ship there, which they very much wanted." Blackbeard made a special point of terrorizing captives from New England, because the only two surviving crewmembers of his old friend Sam Bellamy were languishing in the Boston Prison. Blackbeard's men warned their captives that if "any of their fellow pirates suffer [in Boston] that they will revenge it on them."

Dissuaded from sailing to Boston by reports of two large Royal Navy frigates said to be based in Boston Harbor, where they were on the lookout for pirates, Blackbeard, Bonnet, and their crewmen decided to head southward. Contrary to several popular accounts, Blackbeard did not stop at the Bahamas en route to the Caribbean, nor did he meet up with Hornigold, who was sailing north in a large sloop confusingly named the *Bonnet*. Blackbeard had so terrorized the coast that his crew was now being credited with a large number of attacks that they could not possibly have taken part in. More trustworthy accounts place them hundreds or even thousands of miles away at the time. Some of these attacks may have been carried out by Hornigold and other, lesser-known pirates prowling the waters so recently terrorized and then vacated by the *Revenge*.

Further complicating the matter of who really attacked where and when is the fact that Blackbeard now commanded two ships, both of them sloops. One was the *Revenge* and the other was a captured prize. Blackbeard and Hornigold were commanding two sloops each, and because they were widely known to sail together, whenever prizes were taken by any one of their four ships, the surviving victims may have assumed that either Hornigold or Blackbeard was in command.

Blackbeard's goal, like that of Bellamy before him, was to capture a ship large and powerful enough that it would allow his gang to withstand even an attack by a Royal Navy frigate or man-of-war. In his search for a suitable ship, Blackbeard sailed both sloops to the arc of the Windward Islands, which marks the edge of the Caribbean. During their foray, a French slave ship named *La Concorde* came into view. She was a large, swift, powerful vessel, a 250-ton ship-rigged slaver, with a strong oak hull and enough gun ports to accommodate up to forty cannons. She would have presented fearsome opposition to the pirates except for the fact that over seventy percent of her crew was dead or incapacitated by illness and unable to fight back. Blackbeard's two sloops easily captured the nearly defenseless slaver. Blackbeard now had the flagship he had so long desired to lead his growing armada. He refitted the slave ship and renamed her the *Queen Anne's Revenge*.

Blackbeard transferred all of his loot and personal effects from the *Revenge* to the *Queen Anne's Revenge*, along with his choice of the most able crewmen and some of the cannons. Stede Bonnet, for his part, had by now largely recovered from his wounds; despite his inexperience, Blackbeard allowed him to resume command of the *Revenge* and a crew of about fifty men. But Blackbeard made it abundantly clear that the return of the ship was contingent on the condition that Bonnet defer completely to his command and go wherever he ordered him to go.

With a tremendous warship and two sloops at his command, Blackbeard now unleashed a piratical rampage ranging from the Bay of Honduras to the Bahamas. The pirate flotilla captured and plundered somewhere in the neighborhood of sixteen ships, several of which the pirates destroyed. While on their campaign of terror and robbery, the pirates made two of their prizes into consort ships and scuttled one of their tired old sloops. Blackbeard was now commodore of an armada of four ships, boasting more than sixty cannons and a complement of almost seven hundred men.

While these ships and crewmen were a mighty force, they were also hugely expensive to keep supplied and maintained. Blackbeard needed a valuable target, and the hit-or-miss nature of merchant shipping was simply too unpredictable to meet his needs. Consequently, he resolved to blockade the busiest, most important port in the southern colonies of America—the harbor town of Charleston, South Carolina. The blockade of Charleston is discussed in detail in the chapter on Blackbeard, so we will simply say here that the city was terrified as the infamous pirate's flotilla blockaded the harbor and captured any ships attempting to sail into or out of Charleston. If that were not enough, the vessels trained their great guns on the city and forced its unconditional surrender. They took everything they wanted, and the citizens met their every demand.

During the blockade of Charleston, Teach learned from captured crews that Captain Woodes Rogers had been installed as the new governor of Nassau under the condition that he put an end to the pirate threat plaguing the Caribbean. Supporting him in his mission was a squadron of British warships. Once installed in office, Rogers offered amnesty and pardon to any and all pirates who agreed to retire and give up their buccaneering raids on merchant shipping; those who refused would be mercilessly hunted down, captured, and hanged. In fact, Blackbeard's old friend and former captain, Benjamin Hornigold, had wisely accepted this pardon and was recommending that all of his brethren along the coast do the same.

Faced with this growing threat to his livelihood, Teach began to think seriously about breaking up his own company. In June 1718, he eased the *Queen Anne's Revenge* into Topsail Inlet (now Beaufort, North Carolina) and deliberately ran her hard into the shoals along with a second ship commanded by Israel Hands. Both vessels stuck fast in the Carolina sands and were damaged beyond repair. Blackbeard then informed his unhappy guest, Captain Stede Bonnet, of his intention to accept the king's pardon but magnanimously turned the *Revenge* over to her former master, suggesting that he too accept the pardon. Bonnet traveled in a small sloop to Bath, North Carolina, and secured his pardon from Governor Eden before returning to Topsail Inlet, only to find that Blackbeard had sailed away in the remaining sloop, the *Adventure*. Surprisingly true to his word, Blackbeard had left the *Revenge* waiting for Bonnet's return, but his men had stripped her of all valuables, and she possessed only the bare minimum crew necessary to sail her. The rest of the assembled crewmen from Blackbeard's flotilla had sailed off with the infamous old rogue.

Bonnet made sail with the intention of heading south to St. Thomas in the West Indies to secure a Dutch privateering commission against the Spanish. On his way out, however, he encountered twenty-five sailors whom Blackbeard had marooned on a small, sandy island, devoid of food, water, or vegetation. Bonnet rescued them only to learn that Blackbeard and the rest of the crewmen, not to mention all the loot and booty, were headed toward Ocracoke Inlet, North Carolina. Enraged by the deception, theft, and betrayal, Bonnet set off in pursuit, but he never saw his cunning companion and captor again. After cruising for four days without success, Bonnet reluctantly directed the *Revenge* toward Virginia.

Off the Virginia coast, the *Revenge* encountered a pink laden with stock and provisions. The crew on the *Revenge* seized her and took a dozen or so barrels of pork and four hundred weight of bread. Reminded by his crewmen that he had accepted the king's pardon and, as such, should be careful of any actions that might be seen as piracy, Bonnet decided to "trade" for what he had just stolen. In due course, he returned the pink to its owner and added eight casks of rice and an old cable as "payment."

The captain and crew of the *Revenge* may have actually wanted to renounce their illegal ways, but a severe lack of money and supplies, thanks to Blackbeard's pillaging of their ship, put them in a desperate situation and made becoming honest men a difficult proposition. They pursued and captured a sixty-ton sloop off Cape Henry only two days later, a prize laden with rum and molasses. Bonnet had no money to pay for the goods and no ability to post security. Consequently, the crew unanimously decided they would all return to piracy. They kept the sloop and transferred eight experienced crewmen aboard to take command of her. Considering that, as the saying goes, pirates will always be pirates, it should not have come as a surprise when Bonnet awoke the next morning to find that the eight sailors had quietly slipped away during the night, stealing the stolen ship. He never heard from them again.

Stede Bonnet's luck as a pirate was as dismal as his leadership and lack of sailing ability. Frustrated by the poor prey off the Virginia Capes, he now turned north to the Delaware Bay. There he took a few small ships, but none of them carried much in the way of booty. At the end of July, he departed the Delaware for the Cape Fear River in the Carolinas. Here he gave the *Revenge* a new name, the *Royal James*, and spent several months refitting her and repairing her well-traveled hull. Word spread to the surrounding area that a notorious pirate captain and his band of cutthroats were hiding out in the meandering waterways of Cape Fear. From the port of Charleston, Governor Robert Johnson sent two heavily armed sloops to check out the rumors. The sloops sailed into the mouth of the river, trapping the newly christened *Royal James*.

Bonnet decided to make a run for it, but when the sloops maneuvered to cut off his escape, he unintentionally ran the *Royal James* aground. An exchange of fire ensued, and his crew suffered heavy losses. The survivors were captured and taken as prisoners to Charleston, where the victory over the notorious pirates proved to be the cause of great public celebration.

Stede Bonnet and his men were held prisoner in Charleston, despite the fact that no proper prison had yet been built. The authorities hoped the captive pirates would provide evidence that could be used against Blackbeard, Hornigold, and other pirates, but instead of cooperating, Bonnet and a few of his crewmen made a daring escape, only to be recaptured on Sullivan's Island.

An admiralty court was convened and all the captured pirates were tried, declared guilty, and sentenced to death. Surprisingly, a significant effort was made to save Bonnet from execution. He had friends in Charleston, and they lobbied vigorously to have him sent to England, where his case could be reviewed by the king. But the expense would have been considerable, and his guilt was so unquestionable that the result was unlikely to change the verdict. He was guilty and there was no evidence to the contrary. Stede Bonnet was sent to the gallows on November 16, 1718, in a pitiful state after a vain, begging appeal in writing to Judge Nicholas Trot, who had sentenced him to death. The wealthy gentleman planter from Barbados had wanted to become an infamous pirate captain, and he met the end of most infamous pirate captains—dancing the Tyburn jig at the end of the hangman's noose.

Bartholomew "Black Bart" Roberts and Walter Kennedy

With the death of Blackbeard, a brief respite from the pirate plague settled gently across the Virginia coast. Nevertheless, the threat of a fresh wave of piracy remained a real and lingering menace to the Chesapeake region and the entire Eastern Seaboard. Less than a year after the Battle of Ocracoke, more than seventy pirate crews were actively plundering the shipping lanes off the North American coast, and Spanish privateers were ceaselessly wreaking havoc on British colonial trade.

Following this first concerted crackdown on piracy, there had been an unspoken but perceptible shift in the attitude of the loosely knit brethren of the pirate community. The most noticeable change in their freebooting practices seems to have been a willingness to declare open war on all honest men in revenge for those brethren who fell to the forces of law and order. It was no longer a case of privateering against ships of certain nations. This new breed of pirates, including men like Sam Bellamy and Blackbeard, would attack anyone, for any reason—or for no reason—so long as they thought they could get away with it and there might be the slightest opportunity for plunder. They pitted themselves in opposition to all established mores, laws, and authorities. It was a case of outlaws versus the world.

On the other hand, some successful pirates, flush with plunder, loot, and booty, seemed perfectly happy to retire to a comfortable life on land before they met the inevitable violent end at sea or dangling at the end of the hangman's rope. Many of those who retired lacked the common sense or discipline necessary to disguise their ill-gotten fortunes and were easily spotted by the authorities. For Governor Alexander Spotswood of Virginia, these changes in style and objective reinvigorated his determination to see every individual associated with piracy brought to justice in the court and on the gallows.

The terror of Blackbeard may have passed, but in the spring of 1720, Virginia once again had the opportunity to dispense justice and punishment to another raucous band of pirates. These brigands were former crewmen of a company commanded by one of the most notorious and successful of all oceangoing brigands—none other than the dread pirate Captain Bartholomew "Black Bart" Roberts. In this case, however, justice would not be served by a valorous hand such as that of Lieutenant Maynard, but rather through the resourceful self-control of a most unlikely individual—a gentle, pacifistic Quaker merchant captain named Luke Knott.

Although he may well have been the most successful pirate in history, Bartholomew Roberts, like Luke Knott, was a most unlikely candidate for his role in life. Tall and handsome, with flowing black locks tumbling across his shoulders and a penchant for flamboyant clothes, Roberts was well read, well spoken, and an upright and moral man in virtually all respects. By all accounts, he did not swear, gamble, or drink strong liquor, nor would he tolerate those who did.

This future pirate king was born in Pembrokeshire, Wales, around 1682, at the dawn of the Golden Age of Piracy, and christened with the rather ordinary name of John Roberts. Virtually nothing is known of his early life, but he probably went to sea at the tender age of thirteen or fourteen, when he signed on to a merchant ship as cabin boy. Twenty-three or twenty-four years later, in 1719, the now thirty-seven-year-old Roberts had risen to the rank of third mate on a British slave trader named the *Princess*. Having no political connections or family money with which to buy a commission, there was little chance Roberts's career would advance any further, and his wages probably would not have increased much beyond their current three pounds sterling per month. Had fate not intervened, Roberts undoubtedly would have remained a penniless junior officer for the rest of his working life.

In early June 1719, while the *Princess* was anchored off the Gold Coast of Africa waiting to pick up her next load of tragic human cargo, she was attacked and captured by two pirate ships, the *Royal Rover* and the *Royal James*. Although the *Princess* had little of value to steal, a number of her crew members were taken prisoner and impressed into service aboard the shorthanded pirate vessels. One of the captives was third mate John Roberts.

Although understandably furious at being captured, Roberts must have been shocked to find that his captors were led by a fellow Welshman and Pembrokeshire native, Howell Davis. By all accounts, Captain Davis was a fair man, at least for a pirate, and the democratic way he ran his two ships impressed Roberts. Howell, in turn, was impressed by Roberts's natural leadership abilities, discipline, charm, and education. Adding to their bond was the fact that they were the only two men on board who could speak Welsh, and Davis quickly made Roberts his confidant, sharing things in their native tongue that he did not want spread among the crew in general. Roberts proved his value to Davis by demonstrating a high level of navigational abilities, and the captain quickly promoted him to chief navigator of the *Royal Rover*.

Only five weeks after Roberts joined Davis's crew, the *Royal James* began leaking because of extensive worm damage and had to be abandoned. Packing his entire crew onto the *Royal Rover*, Davis sailed to Principe Island, where he hoisted a British flag and was allowed to enter the harbor. Never one to allow an opportunity for making a bit of easy money to slip away, Davis invited the governor of Principe aboard his ship for a luncheon. In truth, Davis planned to take the governor prisoner and hold him for ransom. The governor had learned of the pirates' true identity and accepted the invitation, but he invited Davis to first come to the fort for a glass of wine before lunch. When Davis's longboat pulled up to the docks, he was met by a guard of honor, but as they escorted their guest toward the fort, the soldiers turned their muskets on Davis and his men, shooting them dead.

Having witnessed the murders of their captain and shipmates, the pirates still on board maneuvered the *Royal Rover* out of the harbor and into the safety of the open water as fast as they could, swearing that they would have their revenge. The first order of business, however, was to elect a new captain. In one of the most sudden and spectacular rises in command in naval history, John Roberts was elected captain of the *Royal Rover* by an almost unanimous vote after only six weeks as a member of the crew. Stunned as he may have been, Roberts justified accepting the position by reportedly saying, "It is better to be a commander than a common man, since I have dipped my hands in muddy water and must be a pirate."

To satisfy the crew's demand for revenge, Roberts's first act as captain was to take the *Royal Rover* back to Principe, where they made a daring nighttime attack, murdering a large portion of the island's male population and stealing everything of value and hauling it back to the ship. With the score nicely settled for the death of their captain and crewmates, Roberts turned his attention to the business of running his ship. Instantly marking himself as a very different kind of captain, Roberts made the unprecedented move of allowing his crew to decide where the *Royal Rover* would go next. The two options he offered were the East Indies or Brazil. The vote was for Brazil.

Before reaching Brazil, Roberts and his men attacked and captured a Dutch and an English slave trader within a span of seventy-two hours. There is no record of whether either ship was carrying slaves at the time, but Roberts looted everything of value, set the crews adrift in longboats, traded his sloop for one of the captured ships, and burned the sloop and the remaining slaver.

It seems that during the remainder of the trip to South America, Captain John Roberts spent much of his time reinventing himself. Like many pirates, he adopted an alias, becoming Bartholomew Roberts. Bolstering his new image as a pirate captain, Roberts adopted what would become his invariable wardrobe with items looted from the captured slave ships. Henceforth, Bart Roberts always appeared wearing a crimson waistcoat and matching breeches, his hat decorated with a flowing crimson plume, and two pairs of pistols slung from silk bandoliers crossing his chest. Like all pirates, Roberts needed a distinctive flag, and as though to declare his resignation to having a merry if predictably short life, Roberts's flag displayed figures of himself and death holding an hourglass between them. Or possibly the flag was a warning that time was running out for the future victims of Bartholomew Roberts.

The *Royal Rover* reached Brazil in early July 1719, but after nine weeks of fruitless traveling, the pirates' hoped-for bounty of merchant ships had failed to appear. Roberts considered moving on to the West Indies, but before he could make a final decision, they spotted a convoy of forty-two fully laden Portuguese merchantmen massed just outside Todos de Santos Bay. Always wary of pirates, the Portuguese routinely formed large flotillas that were escorted back to Europe by heavily armed warships. But the warships were far behind the main contingent, and the merchantmen were only lightly armed. Still, there were three and a half dozen of them, and only a fool would attack so many ships at once.

In an amazing display of audacious courage, Roberts concealed his cannons and allowed his ship to drift casually into the midst of the Portuguese. With an air of casual friendliness, Roberts invited a random Portuguese captain to join him for dinner and drinks. He welcomed the captain aboard with all due respect and then explained to his guest that he was now a prisoner, but that he, his ship, and his crew would be unharmed if he revealed which ship among the flotilla carried the richest cargo. Reluctantly, the captain cooperated.

Roberts sailed alongside his intended victim, with its 150-man crew and forty guns. He unleashed a withering broadside and took the ship with the loss of only two men. Before the other Portuguese ships could come to their companion's aid, Roberts's men had removed a cargo of sugar, tobacco, and furs; forty thousand gold coins; a large quantity of jewelry and precious stones; and a priceless diamond-studded gold cross destined for the king of Portugal. The haul was, in every sense, worth a king's ransom. The bulk of the treasure would be divided among the crew, but Roberts kept the diamond cross for himself.

Giddy with success, the pirates sought a safe haven in which to luxuriate and divide the spoils. They decided to head for Suriname and made landfall at Devil's Island (destined to become an infamous French prison in centuries to come). The Dutch governor of Suriname received them civilly, and according to some accounts, Roberts presented him with the diamond cross. This magnanimous bribe would have ensured a lifetime of favor and safe harbor on the islands, but it may have been a simple case of not knowing how to divide a diamond-studded cross among a gang of cutthroats. Other accounts claim that Roberts retained the cross for himself and kept it until his dying day. Whatever may have happened to the cross, the populace of Suriname was universally friendly to the pirates, and their women "exchanged wares and drove a considerable trade with them." This could have been a euphemism for prostitution, or it may have plainly meant commerce; we simply don't know.

While ensconced on Suriname, Roberts learned from an American sloop that a brigantine from Rhode Island with a cargo of provisions was due shortly. The pirates sighted her one afternoon, and Roberts set off with forty men in the small sloop to bring her in. Luck was not with them, however; the sloop lost the wind and drifted aimlessly for eight days before being able to return to the *Royal Rover's* last known position. But the *Royal Rover* had disappeared. Apparently, Walter Kennedy, who had been put in temporary command during Roberts's absence, had absconded with the ship and its fabulous cargo of loot. Furious at the betrayal, Roberts, his diminished crew, and their little sloop, now renamed the *Royal Fortune*, doggedly set out for Brazil.

In "grievous passion," Roberts and his forty remaining crewmen plotted a new future. They would rebuild their wealth and fortune and revenge themselves on Walter Kennedy when the opportunity presented itself. They drew up a set of articles that all would sign and swear to as a means of ensuring some degree of loyalty to each other, "excluding ALL Irishmen from the benefit of it, to whom they had an implacable Aversion on account of Kennedy." All current and future crew members had to agree to follow the articles if they wished to remain aboard the *Royal Fortune*. Those who did not agree were welcome to leave the ship at the next port of call.

Almost all pirate articles were fairer than the rules imposed on military ships of the day, but Roberts's articles were notable in what they did not allow. No gambling, either with dice or cards, was allowed on board the ship. No swearing was allowed. All lights were to be put out promptly at eight o'clock in the evening. No cabin boys or women were allowed on ship; any man found to have brought a woman on board was to be executed. Sunday was to be observed as the Sabbath, and even the ship's musicians were excused from working on the Lord's Day. No fighting was allowed on the ship; if any of the men had a quarrel, they were to wait until the ship docked, and then they could fight, with swords or pistols, until first blood was drawn. No one was allowed to suggest breaking up the ship's company until they had taken at least 1,000 pounds sterling for each crewman. Roberts's articles may have raised some eyebrows among his crew, but no one left the ship and they all agreed to sign.

If Roberts's articles seem puritanical for pirates, the rules he imposed on himself were even more stringent. Captain Roberts was invariably respectful of women and clergymen, he rarely used profanity, and although he may occasionally have drunk a mug of beer or a glass of wine, he never touched hard liquor and preferred tea to any other beverage. Most peculiar of all, when the captain of a captured ship proved cooperative, Roberts would sometimes offer him a small gift of appreciation before sending him and his crew on their way in a state of stunned amazement.

Following the remarkably bold Portuguese incident, the name of Bartholomew Roberts spread across the Caribbean. The French, Portuguese, Spanish, and Dutch all posted bounties on Roberts, and the islands of Martinique and Barbados each equipped two pirate hunters and sent them out specifically to search for the *Royal Fortune*. The Barbadian ships caught up with their quarry, and on February 26, 1720, they cornered the *Royal Fortune* traveling in the company of another pirate vessel. The *Royal Fortune*'s companion fled the scene, and Roberts's ship took heavy damage and lost twenty men before escaping to Charlestown, capital of the tiny island of Nevis in the Leeward Islands.

Outraged by his hair's-breadth escape, Roberts vowed vengeance against his adversaries and designed a new flag bearing his figure standing atop two skulls, one marked ABH (A Barbadian's Head) and the other AMH (A Martiniquian's Head). It was the beginning of a marked change in the demeanor of the polite, courteous Captain Bartholomew Roberts. But revenge would have to wait; for the moment, it was too dangerous to remain in the Caribbean. Roberts decided that North America might offer fresh opportunities and far less danger than the West Indies.

Electing to begin his next series of raids as far as possible from his enemies, Roberts took advantage of the fine summer weather and headed to the far north. When he reached Cape Breton, Nova Scotia, he paused long enough to capture two ships before continuing northward to Newfoundland, where he raided the harbor of Ferryland and seized an even dozen ships, plundering and burning the lot. On June 21, 1720, the *Royal Fortune* reached the seaside town of Trepassy, where it sailed boldly into the ship-filled harbor with its Jolly Roger flying for all to see and the entire crew assembled on deck, some blowing trumpets and others beating on drums. As the crews of twenty-two ships in Trepassy Harbor and startled civilians on the quayside stared in wonder, Roberts unleashed a withering barrage of cannon fire. In a panic, the crews fled their ships, jumping into the water to save themselves from being blown to pieces. With the ships free for the taking, the crew of the *Royal Fortune* aimed her guns toward the town, holding its small garrison at bay while Roberts's men looted one ship after another, moving the captured cargo to a fine English-made brig carrying sixteen guns. When every ship had been stripped of valuables, the pirates transferred their possessions and booty from the *Royal Fortune* to the fresh, new brig. After torching or sinking every other ship in the harbor, the *Royal Fortune* ended her career after she and the brig turned their guns on Trepassy, nearly destroying the entire town. With their fury vented, the pirates burned the old *Royal Fortune*, took to their new ship, and sailed out of sight.

The attack on Trepassy was followed by a month of the most furious, relentless, and devastating series of pirate raids in naval history. In addition to capturing 150 fishing boats and 26 sloops, Roberts ran down and captured an eighteen-gun galley and a twenty-eight-gun French bark. He kept the bark and christened her the new *Royal Fortune*. With this new ship, the pirates took eight to ten more ships, including another French bark, which they fitted with twenty-six guns and named the *Good Fortune*. Knowing when a graceful exit was in order, Bartholomew Roberts headed south by mid-July, leaving Newfoundland a smoking wreck. There is no exact tally of how many ships he took during his six weeks in the far north, but the total is between 206 and 210 craft of all sizes. No other captain, ship, or crew has approached this number of captures in such a short period of time.

Roberts did not attack another ship until he reached the Virginia Colony, where, after capturing a merchant vessel, he again headed south, toward the harbor of Charleston in the Carolinas. But a raging storm drove him back northward, until the *Royal Fortune* and *Good Fortune* finally managed to dock at Cape May, New Jersey. Unbeknownst to Roberts, word of the Newfoundland devastation had reached

British authorities in New England, where the governor felt a grudging admiration for Roberts's boldness but immediately notified coastal towns and ships to be on the lookout for the pirates.

By the time Roberts sailed into Cape May, the locals already knew his ships' identity and sent word to the authorities. While local ships assembled for an attack on the *Royal Fortune* and *Good Fortune*, the Royal Navy blockaded the port to prevent the pirates' escape. Roberts realized he was surrounded and attempted to force his way through the massed ships and a hail of cannon fire. In the ensuing melee, the *Royal Fortune* took too many hits to remain afloat, and as the surviving crew swam toward the *Good Fortune*, their crippled ship—her holds bulging with gold, silver, and other valuable goods—sank beneath the waters of Delaware Bay.

By late August 1720, the *Good Fortune* had taken another prize, which Roberts used to replace the lost *Royal Fortune*, and the two ships found safe harbor on the Caribbean island of Carriacou, near Grenada. While resupplying and refitting his ships, Roberts renamed the *Good Fortune* the *Royal Rover* and dubbed the new acquisition the *Good Fortune*. The ships moved on to St. Bartholomew Island, where the governor proved amenable to having pirates in his port, and Roberts allowed his crew several weeks of shore leave.

But the lure of the sea and plunder pulled them back to the water, and by the beginning of October, they were on their way to St. Lucia, taking more than a dozen French and English ships along the way. The pirates' next stop was at St. Kitts, where they planned another shore leave, but an invitation to the governor to share a meal on the *Royal Rover* was met with a stern rebuff and the threat that if they did not leave at once, both ships would be attacked. To prove their point, local forces fired several warning shots from the fort. Shocked at this unseemly display of bad manners, Roberts seized one ship from its berth and burned two others before taking to the sea. For reasons known only to Bartholomew Roberts, before leaving port he sent an aggrieved letter to the governor complaining that "had you come off as you ought to have done and drank a glass of wine with me and my company I should not [have] harmed the least vessel in your harbor. Further it is not your guns you fired that affrighted me or hindered our coming ashore, but the wind not proving to our expectation that hindered it." Roberts went on, complaining of the loss of his ships at various places and the horrid way those of his men who had been taken prisoner were being treated. Evidently, Roberts thought his letter may not have made his point strongly enough, so the next day he took his ships back into the harbor at St. Kitts, where they plundered fifteen French and English ships before the locals drove them off with cannon fire from the fort and guard ships.

By January 1721, Roberts had added a third ship to his navy. This one was a Dutch slaver to which he added thirty-two cannons. With three ships to aid him, Roberts began taking revenge against Martinique for having sent ships against him the previous year. He sent the Dutch ship into Martinique Harbor, instructing a messenger to spread the word of a profitable slave auction about to be held on St. Lucia. Moving his other two ships into position off St. Lucia, he seized and looted an entire convoy of fourteen French ships when they arrived from Martinique. The pirates mercilessly tortured those they took prisoner, and many of the men died at the hands of Roberts's pirates. Taking his pick among the French ships, Roberts retained an eighteen-gun brigantine and burned the remaining thirteen ships. The take may have been satisfying, but Roberts's next prize offered up an unexpected bounty. The ship was a fifty-two-gun French man-of-war, and among the passengers was the same governor of Martinique who had ordered two ships to hunt down Roberts. The pirates seized the ship as a prize and hanged the governor from a yardarm, where he dangled as a warning to all who would oppose "Black Bart" Roberts.

Now in possession of more ships than he could crew, Roberts eliminated those he did not need and reduced his fleet to the three most serviceable and formidable vessels. The new fleet consisted of the fifty-two-gun French man-of-war, renamed the *Royal Fortune*; a bark named the *Fortune*; and a barkentine named the *Good Fortune*. In many respects, it was the finest contingent of pirate ships ever assembled. But while Roberts's collection of ships and treasure flourished, and his attacks had nearly brought shipping in the West Indies to a halt, he was having a serious problem controlling the more than five hundred fractious pirates who now served under him. There were rumblings of desertion and perhaps even mutiny.

Angry and frustrated, Roberts insisted he was not afraid of any of them. He invited any man who questioned his authority to go ashore and fight him with their choice of pistols or swords. In his diary, he commented that pirates elected a man to the captaincy only in order to tyrannize over him. None of his men accepted the invitation to fight their captain, but on April 20, 1721, Thomas Anstis, who was commanding the *Good Fortune*, stole away in the night, leaving Roberts with only two ships and a burning hatred for the treachery of men whom he had made rich beyond their wildest dreams.

It was the second time Bart Roberts had had a ship stolen by one of his officers, and he swore it would be the last. Exhausted, angry, frustrated, and hunted by every nation with possessions in the Caribbean, Roberts turned the *Royal Fortune* and *Fortune* eastward and headed back toward Africa, where he had begun his career as a pirate less than two years earlier.

Let us leave Captain Bartholomew Roberts as he sails off into the east in search of further glory and riches and turn our attention to Walter Kennedy, the man who stole Roberts's *Rover* and its load of Portuguese treasure in August 1719. There is no surviving record of how or why Kennedy and his men came to the decision to mutiny against the bold and dreaded Captain Roberts, but Kennedy seemed to the mutineers a logical choice for the captaincy of the *Rover*. By all accounts, he was a brave man who had often proven himself in combat under Roberts's flag.

Unfortunately, popularity and courage do not necessarily equate to great leadership; try as he might, Walter Kennedy could not get the crew of mutineers to come to a consensus as to their next objective. Some were for continuing with piracy and plundering, but the majority—undoubtedly encouraged by the enormous amount of treasure in their ship's hold—were for dividing the booty and making for home the best way possible. Finally they reached an accord: the crew would disband, they would divide the loot, and after that it would be each man for himself.

Their first problem was disposing of the Portuguese prize of tobacco, sugar, and hides. This they graciously turned over to a New England sea captain named Cane, the master of a sloop they had once captured in the Suriname River. The elated Captain Cane made his way to Antigua, where he found a welcoming and profitable market for the commodities from his newly acquired stolen ship. After receiving his cut from Captain Cane, Kennedy set the *Rover* on a course for the West Indies and the island of Barbados. During this voyage, they encountered several English vessels, each of which the pirates seized, stripped of her goods and provisions, and released.

Kennedy's meanderings about the West Indies had drawn attention in the colonial newspapers, one of which noted, "the Pyrates are very rife about that Island [of Barbados] and other parts of the West Indies, and doe a great deal of Damage, taking several vessels . . . some they plunder, and others they carry away." But everything was about to change for Captain Kennedy, as he now called himself, and his band of opportunistic deserters.

Just after New Year's Day 1720, Kennedy found himself near Barbados, where he encountered "a very peaceable ship belonging to Virginia" called the *West River Merchant*. The 150-ton merchantman was lightly manned by a crew of only about a dozen or so sailors and was bound from London to Virginia via the West Indies. She was captained by an unlikely figure for a merchant captain cruising pirate-infested waters. His name was Luke Knott, and he was a devout, God-fearing, peace-loving Quaker. Unlike most merchant captains sailing troubled waters, Knott strictly forbade any type of arms aboard his *West River Merchant*. She carried neither cannons nor pistols, and her crewmen were not even armed with swords, cutlasses, or fighting knives. Facing the threat of assault by a heavily armed and well-manned pirate ship boasting thirty-two cannons, twenty-seven swivel guns, and a company of 148 men, as well as her well-armed consort, Captain Knott peaceably surrendered to Kennedy.

After boarding the *West River Merchant*, the pirates began rummaging the hold for loot. Fortunately for Knott and his men, the pirates found little of interest other than a few provisions. Captain Knott's passive and almost pleasant cooperation, however, had a marked impression on Kennedy and his men. Several among their number saw an opportunity to finally take their share of the booty and use the Quaker's ship to slip unnoticed back into society. The pirates offered Knott compensation for the provisions they removed, which totaled about 250 pounds sterling. Next, Kennedy "obliged Knot to take 8 of his Men on board his Ship, and made him give an Obligation under his Hand, that he Ship'd them as Passengers from London, to Virginia." Knott agreed without complaint. He had, in fact, little choice in the matter.

The eight pirates—William Williams, Tobias Butler, William Lake, William Farrow, Daniel Degat, William Pomeroy, Thomas Hall, and

Peter Minshal—took from the *Rover* their share of the plundered loot: a sizable quantity of gold dust, a large number of gold and silver coins, and three African men and one boy as valuable slaves. Kennedy also provided his departing crewmen with a boat, directing Knott to make it available to them "when they required it, to help go from his Ship." In addition, he sent two Portuguese sailors taken prisoner at Todos Santos, as well as two Jews, along on Knott's ship to be set ashore in Virginia.

Having accepted Kennedy's commission, the *West River Merchant* was released to undertake her taxi errand up the Chesapeake. But Captain Knott had little intention of merely playing the role of coerced ferryman. According to later testimony, the pirates on board his ship "lived a jovial life all the while they were upon their voyage," but for the peace-loving Captain Knott, the trip was one of constant threat and terror. The only possibility of overcoming these unwelcome passengers was to surprise them while they slept, for while awake, they wore their weapons constantly, and Knott feared the pirates might murder his crew and seize his ship. Even so, Knott was unlikely to have tried to expel the pirates by force even if he had wanted to. He clung to his staunch Quaker principles and had confidence that his willpower, cunning, and trust in God and his men would help him endure the ordeal.

By the end of the first week of February 1720, the *West River Merchant* arrived at the Virginia Capes, but before she reached Hampton Roads, the wind turned westerly and forced her to drop anchor. Taking advantage of the temporary respite, four of the pirates went to Knott and demanded that they be allowed to launch their boat. Knott happily agreed. The boat shoved off and the four pirates rowed away, bound for Maryland. Just then, however, a frosty February storm hit, forcing them into Back River, "an obscure place at the mouth of York River." It was later reported:

> As soon as they came ashore, their first care was to find a tavern, where they might ease themselves of their heavy golden luggage. They soon found a place to their mind, where for some time they lived very profusely treating all that came into their Company, and there being in the house English Women Servants, who had the good fortune by some Hidden Charms, to appear pleasing to these Picaroons, they set them [the women]

Free, giving their Master 30 Pound, the price he demanded for their time.

The pirates spent generously and liberally at the public house, and with their new "wives" now in tow, indulged in all forms of merriment and debauchery. But in doing so, they had committed an egregious error—they lived extravagantly, and their extravagance attracted attention. Local authorities concluded that these men were not the simple English immigrants they pretended to be. Within a few days of their arrival, the high-living strangers found themselves prisoners in the county jail, held on suspicions of piracy.

Meanwhile, their four companions who were still on Knott's boat remained intent on traveling to Blackbeard's old pirate haven in North Carolina. They stayed with Captain Knott until the storm subsided and he was free to sail peacefully into the James River and dock at Hampton. Although these pirates may have possessed greater patience than their incarcerated comrades, they were certainly no wiser, and as soon as they reached shore they launched into riotous debauchery. While the pirates reveled, Captain Knott went to see Governor Spotswood and informed him "what kind of passengers he had been obliged to bring with him." The governor ordered the immediate arrest of all eight suspected cutthroats. His orders were carried out, and the retired pirates were reunited behind bars within days of setting foot onshore.

All eight of the pirates were put on trial for their crimes by the Virginia Vice Admiralty Court in late 1720. The primary witnesses brought for the prosecution were the two captured Portuguese seamen taken during the robbery of the convoy and recently delivered to safety by Captain Knott. Unable to speak English, they had been obliged to fend for themselves, without resources, until they encountered the captain of an English vessel who happened to speak Portuguese. They told him their tale and now, with the English captain translating, retold their harrowing experiences to the court.

As the trial progressed, the defendants readily admitted that they had been aboard the *Rover* but claimed they had been forced to become pirates after being captured on the Guinea coast. The Portuguese were asked if the pirates seem to be acting "under constraint." They replied "that they appeared as forward in Action, and were busy in Plundering as any of the Crew, and that one of the Prisoners at the Bar, took in a Particular Gold Ring from the Wife of one of the two Portuguese sailors." Further damning evidence was offered by passengers from the *West River Merchant* as well as by Captain Knott himself.

When their turn came to speak, the defendants made a less-than-favorable impression. Governor Spotswood described six of the eight defendants as "the most profligate Wretches I ever heard of, for, as they behaved themselves with the greatest impudence at the Bar, they were no sooner taken from it than they vented their imprecations on their judges and all concerned in their prosecution, and vowed if they were again at liberty they would spare none alive that should fall into their hands."

The trial concluded with the inevitable guilty sentence. Of the eight condemned criminals, six of them would be executed. The four who had served as officers and had been most active in the attack and seizure of merchants' ships—and who had been the most offensive and threatening during the trial—would be hanged and their bodies hung in chains as a warning to others with a penchant for lawlessness. Two others who had been more respectful during the trial would be hanged a week later but would be granted the "liberty to be buried." The six pirates who had been sentenced to death showed no signs of remorse or repentance. The governor's council recommended a pardon for the remaining two, William Lake and Peter Minshal, both of whom "shew'd a just Abhorrence of their past Crimes" and behaved during the trial with civility. With the support of Spotswood, the two defendants were sentenced to serve on board one of the guard ships on the Virginia Station.

Predictably, the recovery of the stolen loot the pirates had brought ashore became a legal mess. They had hidden most of it somewhere along the coast, and although the government eventually recovered between 1,500 and 2,000 pounds sterling in gold and silver, this accounted for only about one-eighth of what the pirates were known to have taken with them.

For his part in bringing the pirates to justice, Captain Knott received praise and official commendation for bravery and calmness in action. Had he behaved otherwise, it would have been highly unlikely that any of his crewmen would have survived the journey, and there would have been no witnesses to testify against the pirates. The government also compensated Knott for the loss of his merchandise from the recovered loot.

The execution of the six pirates might have seemed to have been the solution to a problem for Virginia, but in fact it set off a chain of events that would pose an even greater threat for Governor Spotswood. When Bartholomew Roberts learned of the hangings, he vowed to take revenge on the Virginia authorities. He apparently felt that these convicted pirates were members of his crew despite the fact that they and Walter Kennedy had deserted and stolen the *Rover* and its hold full of treasure. Or perhaps Roberts felt that Virginia had robbed him of the opportunity to torture and kill the men himself. We will never know for certain. What we do know is that Roberts captured the Virginia-bound *Jeremiah* off Bermuda and charged her master, Captain Turner, with conveying the message that he would be paying Virginia a visit. The message was relayed to Governor Spotswood along with personal threats against both him and Captain Knott. Spotswood was aware of what Roberts had done to towns in the Caribbean and to Trepassy, Newfoundland. Spotswood and the council immediately ordered the Virginia coastline better armed.

The governor ordered the construction of batteries mounting fifty-four guns at the entrances to the Rappahannock, York, and James Rivers. Two lookout posts were established, with one at Cape Henry and another at Cape Charles in Northampton County. Signal beacons were also erected along the coastline so that warnings could be relayed rapidly up the coast as soon as Roberts's black flag was sighted. Spotswood also wrote to the governors of New York, New Jersey, New England, and South Carolina, informing them of the nature of the threat and the might of their foe, as well as requesting that any Royal Navy ships berthed at their stations be sent to reinforce those on the Chesapeake.

Governor Spotswood's fears were magnified when he received word that Roberts had just captured a French warship carrying the governor of the island of Martinique. If Roberts's ability to capture a warship wasn't frightening enough, it was said that the pirates had hanged the governor from the yardarm, while others prisoners who opposed them had their ears cut off or were tied to the mast and used for target practice.

Fortunately for Virginia and her crusading governor, Bartholomew Roberts never returned to Virginia. According to most reports, he was killed in February 1722 in battle with HMS *Swallow*. Other reports suggest that he secretly made his way to Florida with a small fortune after having faked his own death in the battle. Spotswood, however, was not comforted by reports of Roberts's death and spent the rest of his life in fear of pirates and reprisals. Two years after being relieved of his post as governor, Alexander Spotswood had failed to report back to England because he was terrified of boarding a ship, fearing his treatment at the hands of pirates. Writing to the Board of Trade in 1724, Governor Spotswood lamented his lack of "some safe opportunity to get home" to London and insisted that he would travel only in a well-armed man-of-war.

> Your Lordships will easily conceive my Meaning when you reflect on the Vigorous part I've acted to Suppress Pirates: and if those barbarous Wretches can be moved to cut off the Nose & Ears of a Master for but correcting his own Sailors, what inhuman Treatment must I expect, should I fall within their Power, who have been markt as the principle Object of their Vengeance, for cutting off their arch Pirate Thatch, with all his Grand Designs & making so many of their Fraternity to swing in the open air of Virginia.

John Paul Jones

The title of this book is *Pirates of Virginia*, but it might be more accurately called *Pirates IN Virginia*, as the only pirate discussed thus far who was actually from Virginia was William Claiborne, whose story was told in the first chapter. Of the rest, although their travels brought them to Virginia to prey on the rich shipping, none of them stayed for very long—at least not voluntarily. John Paul Jones was also not a native Virginian, nor, in fact, did he spend much of his career in the colony; he was born in Scotland, and although he considered himself an American in every sense, he never established a permanent home here. But if he had considered anywhere in the world to be his home, it would have been Fredericksburg, Virginia. Whether Jones was a pirate depends entirely on your point of view. The British Crown, which held claim to the colonies, certainly thought he was, but the Americans for whom he fought considered him a hero.

John Paul (later known as John Paul Jones) was born at Arbigland, Scotland, on July 6, 1747. His father, also named John Paul, was a gardener and his mother, Jean MacDuff, was the daughter of a farmer in the neighboring parish of New-Abbey. Although not poor, the Pauls were decidedly working-class. Some of John Paul Jones's early biographers refused to accept his humble origins, insisting he was the illegitimate son of the Third Earl of Selkirk. In truth, he was an average boy who overcame class prejudice and succeeded in a world dominated by the rich and powerful.

John was the fourth of seven children. The firstborn was William Paul, who went abroad early in life and settled and married in Fredericksburg, Virginia. It appears that William was the only one of John's siblings with whom he kept close ties. John finished his schooling at twelve and insisted on going to sea, so his parents apprenticed him to local ship owner John Younger. Lacking the social connections necessary for quick advancement, the apprentice committed himself to seven years' service. In 1761, at age thirteen, he made his first trip on the *Friendship* to Fredericksburg, Virginia, where he visited his brother William, who had established a tailor shop there.

A number of voyages between England, the West Indies, and the Chesapeake followed. The next year, John Paul again found himself in Fredericksburg, where he stayed with his brother, reading books and studying navigation. John Paul loved Fredericksburg, felt comfortable there, and hoped that one day he might purchase a home in the bustling town. John Paul came and went with the tides and the shipments until 1764, when Younger went bankrupt and released him from his apprenticeship. Young John Paul then looked for other work to continue his study of seamanship. He took a position as third mate on the *Two Friends*, a ship operating in the African slave trade, which was the most dangerous and least desirable job for a sailor. He could not abide what he called that "abominable trade," but even though he was unhappy in his position, he made the most of it, and in 1768, by the time the twenty-one-year-old left the slaver, he had become its chief mate. Separating from the *Two Friends* in Jamaica, John Paul took passage home on a brig named the *John*. When both the captain and chief mate died of disease en route to Scotland, John Paul was the only person aboard who could navigate, so he assumed command and brought the vessel and its crew of seven safely to Kirkcudbright.

The owners of the *John*, pleased with John Paul's performance, asked him to continue as captain, and for the next two years, he served as master and selling agent for the *John*, making several voyages between Scotland and the West Indies. By 1772, he had graduated to command of the *Betsy*, a large, square-rigged merchant vessel. Through personal initiative, merit, force of character, and luck, in the space of eleven years John Paul had risen from ship's boy to captain. Unlike many of his contemporaries, he did not have his opportunities provided to him; he made his own way and achieved much.

John Paul's life took a dramatic turn in 1773 as a result of his ferocious temper. One of the seamen on the *Betsy*, to whom he later referred to simply as the "ringleader," challenged John Paul's authority and fomented a mutiny when the ship arrived at the West Indian island of Tobago. John Paul confronted the ringleader with a sword, intending, he later claimed, to intimidate the sailor into obedience.

According to John Paul's account, the ringleader then went berserk, picked up a piece of wood, and came at the captain, who defended himself with his sword against repeated blows. Finally John Paul, in self-defense, stabbed his attacker and killed him. If this account is accurate, his subsequent actions seem strange. A few days after the incident, John Paul fled Tobago, traveled incognito to America, and "reinvented" himself. He added a new last name—Jones—probably chosen because it was commonplace. Either Jones's rendition of events leading to the sailor's death were not as he later portrayed them, or the killing of the man, though justifiable, so inflamed the local population that John Paul and his friends feared he would never receive a fair trial.

His recovery from what he later called "that great Misfortune of my Life" was a turning point in Jones's career. While creating the new John Paul Jones, he headed for Fredericksburg, which, he later wrote, had long been his "favorite Country." He intended to settle there permanently and "quit the Sea Service," using money owed him as a merchant captain to "purchase some small tracts of Land." With three thousand inhabitants, the town was a prosperous, bustling port of well-cared-for houses and shady streets. Thomas Jefferson, a frequent visitor to Fredericksburg, wrote, "The town was constantly filled with sailors from all parts of the world."

When the thirteen-year-old John Paul first arrived in Fredericksburg back in 1761, the Rappahannock River valley was lush and verdant. But when the man calling himself John Paul Jones returned in the winter of 1774, he found Fredericksburg cold, gray, and unwelcoming. Worst of all, his older brother had died. Before his death, William Paul had separated from his wife, and the executors named in his will refused to serve. Thus the will could not be executed, and John Paul inherited nothing from his brother's tailoring business.

Jones needed friends and a place to stay, but none of his brother's friends stepped forward. He probably found lodging in one of several boardinghouses or inns. There still stands in Fredericksburg a carefully preserved late-eighteenth-century inn called the Rising Sun, typical of the accommodations available to a traveler of Jones's day. The class divide is stark. As one enters, to the left is a wainscoted room with Queen Anne furniture where the gentlemen ate. Dinner, an ample two-hour affair, cost one shilling and six pence. A private room for the night was one shilling and three pence. To the right is the tavern room, where the barkeep stood behind a wooden enclosure for protection in case the customers became violent. For a penny, a fellow could sleep above the barroom on a straw pallet in a fifteen-by-eighteen-foot room along with fifteen other men, who were required to give the innkeeper their boots at night to keep them from leaving without paying.

There is little doubt Jones would have preferred a gentleman's lodgings. It is true that he was a commoner, but he had shouted commands from the quarterdeck and slept in a captain's cabin. He had no desire to return to the dank intimacy of the lower deck, where the crew slept, their hammocks hanging cheek to cheek. But Jones was short on cash. When he fled Tobago, he had the considerable sum of fifty pounds sterling, but as it turned out, this would have to last him nearly two years.

Serious rumbles of discontent had been rolling through the American colonies in the winter of 1773–74. In December 1773, the Sons of Liberty dressed up like Indians and threw hundreds of crates of tea into Boston Harbor to protest British tax policies. In Virginia, young radicals like Thomas Jefferson, Patrick Henry, and Richard Henry Lee formed a Committee of Correspondence to share their views and experiences with their brethren in the northern colonies. The following September, the First Continental Congress would meet in Philadelphia to take the initial steps on a path that would lead to America's independence from her mother country in less than two years.

But neither rebellious murmurings nor outright defiance against the Crown meant that a social revolution was imminent, at least not yet. All men were not created equal in the Virginia commonwealth, certainly not in the Tidewater region of great estates along the James and Rappahannock Rivers. A "squirearchy" of forty families owned most of the land and kept their subordinates in their place. Gentlemen ate with silver, common folk with a wooden spoon or their fingers.

The outsider John Paul Jones was not welcome in Fredericksburg. He could not count on the goodwill of his brother's friends, because William had been out of favor because of his marital problems, and newly arrived gentlemen from far-off places were expected to present letters of introduction. In eighteenth-century America, strangers were viewed with suspicion and even openly gawked at, particularly when they had a thick Scottish brogue. The landed gentry looked down on Scotsmen, who were seen as crass money-grubbers. In 1781, a wealthy

Virginian named Charles Lee complained that Virginia was becoming a "Mac-ocracy," overrun by a Celtic "banditti."

Jones, however, was welcomed by one group of Virginians—the Freemasons, whose local lodge met regularly at an inn called the Townhouse. Already a member of the brotherhood, Jones was free to attend. Masonry gave its members a sense of exclusivity and gave Jones the social network and sense of belonging he desired. Dr. John K. Read, who was the local grand master, befriended the carefully dressed stranger with a hidden past and a familiar brogue. In a letter he later wrote to Jones, Read reflected on "the many sentimental hours which passed between us at the Grove," a plantation outside Fredericksburg.

During those solitary hours spent in the company of Dr. Read at the Grove, Jones indulged his appetite for reading and thus was obtaining an education. "Any young gentleman traveling through Virginia was presumed to be acquainted with dancing, boxing, card and fiddle-playing and the use of the small sword," wrote Philip Fithian, a Princeton graduate who tutored the sons of Virginia gentry. Jones's lack of skill in these arts proved he was not a gentleman, but gentlemen also prided themselves on their classical learning, and here Jones could catch up. One of his midshipmen later observed, "The learning he obtained . . . from the age of nine years, was from close application to books, of which he was remarkably fond." Jones wished to be, as he later wrote, "a citizen of the world." If he could not join the Virginia landowners, he would transcend them.

But first he wanted to marry one of their daughters. Dorothea Spottswood Dandridge was a dark-haired, dark-eyed beauty of nineteen who came from an established Virginia family. She was the granddaughter of Governor Alexander Spottswood and a cousin of Martha Washington. We do not know much about Jones's courtship of Miss Dandridge, except that he managed to win her heart but not the approval of her father. Jones wrote only that he relinquished "the softer affections of his heart" to go to war. He later learned from Dr. Read that Dorothea had married the governor of Virginia, Patrick Henry. Henry was nearly twice the age of young Dorothea, but he came from a socially acceptable family and was the governor of the colony. According to a biography of Henry, it was known that Dorothea, known as Dolly, "had fancied an impecunious young sailor named John Paul Jones, then visiting cousins on a nearby plantation, but her father dashed her hopes in favor of the more glorious match with the governor." The "cousin" was in all likelihood Dr. Read.

After a year in Virginia, Jones was nearing the end of his savings. He was dependent on Dr. Read's kindness, lodging, and hospitality and appeared to have little or no prospect for employment. But everything was about to change. The declaration of war between the colonies and the Crown saved Jones from his brooding over Miss Dandridge and provided him with a career opportunity.

On April 22, 1775, a horseman rode into Fredericksburg with ominous news. In the dead of night, British marines had removed the gunpowder from the armory at Williamsburg, lest it be seized by rebels. A few days earlier, a British column had marched out to destroy a rebel cache of arms in Concord, Massachusetts, and the colonists resisted. Fighting broke out at Lexington Green and Concord Bridge, and on their retreat to Boston, more than two hundred British redcoats were slain by colonial militia.

Rebellion against the Crown, fueled by hatred of the colonial governors, was boiling over. In March 1775, Governor Patrick Henry thrilled a convention of Virginia delegates by exclaiming, "Give me liberty or give me death!" Predictably, an increasingly nervous British government clamped down on dissenters. On April 29, the streets of Fredericksburg were filled with volunteers, eager to form up and do battle for "liberty." One observer recorded, "We had in this town 600 men in hunting shirts well accoutered that if convinced would have marched to Boston."

Jones witnessed the growing agitation with excitement and an eye for adventure. It is likely that the prospect of war offered him nothing to lose and the whole world to gain. His correspondence included only a high-minded avowal that he relinquished his "prospects for domestic happiness" to "restore peace and goodwill among mankind." Jones's generalities obscure a more particular transformation: war offered Jones a means to social advancement.

In the late summer or early autumn of 1775, Jones traveled to Philadelphia to offer his services to a navy that did not yet exist in a nation that did not exist. In addition to needing a job and social position, Jones had other motives for volunteering. He had plenty to offer the colonial rebels: his seamanship, navigation skills, experience commanding a ship, and knowledge of gunnery. His first ship, the *Friend-*

ship, had carried eighteen guns as protection against French cruisers during the Seven Years' War. As he later wrote, he had made "the Art of War by Sea" his study and had been "fond of a Navy" from his "boyish days up." Serving in the new Continental Navy would allow him to fulfill that childhood dream.

Upon enrolling in the American cause, Jones was commissioned a lieutenant—the "Eldest" or most senior lieutenant in the navy. Jones could have commanded the sloop *Providence* but chose instead to serve as a lieutenant on the flagship of the commander in chief of the Continental Navy, Esek Hopkins, because, Jones said, his "highest Ambition" was to learn from a "Gentleman of Superiour Abilities [and] of superiour Merit." Jones believed he could be immediately useful and would be able to learn more seamanship and fleet maneuvers by serving as a first lieutenant on Hopkins's ship, the *Alfred*, than by commanding his own ship. Throughout his career, Jones made learning and acquiring professional knowledge a priority.

In later years, Jones regretted his decision to sail on the *Alfred* instead of accepting an independent command, which would have given him an opportunity to distinguish himself. The outcome of the *Alfred*'s first operation heightened his dissatisfaction. In 1777, Hopkins's fleet captured the island of New Providence in the Bahamas. Although the operation went smoothly, the governor bought enough time to send away two hundred barrels of gunpowder, whose capture had been the chief object of the expedition.

On its way back from the Bahamas, the fleet sailed to Block Island, Rhode Island, in search of British merchant vessels. Instead, it encountered the British warship HMS *Glasgow*, which should have been easy prey. The American attack was not well coordinated, however, and the *Glasgow* escaped after mauling the American brig *Cabot*. Hopkins's conduct in the encounter with the *Glasgow* convinced Jones that he had nothing to learn from the commander in chief, so when he was again offered command of the *Providence*, Jones jumped at the opportunity.

In August 1776, Jones set sail on his first independent cruise as the privateer captain of the *Providence*. As a commerce raider on this and a subsequent voyage, Jones enjoyed spectacular success. During his first voyage, off the Grand Banks, he captured sixteen prizes and destroyed the local fishing fleet. In his second cruise, again to the Grand Banks, he took several more prizes, including the armed transport *Mellish*. This ship carried a cargo of winter uniforms, which were distributed to the nearly naked Continental Army. As he wrote his friend Joseph Hewes, a delegate to Congress from North Carolina: "In the term of Twelve weeks, including the time of fitting out . . . I took twenty four Prizes." He may have convinced himself that these were acts of patriotism for his adopted country, but Jones was not an American. He was still a British subject. He may have viewed himself as a "citizen of the world," but the Royal Navy saw him as a pirate, a traitor, and an outlaw.

Anticipating that his success would bring promotion to squadron commander, Jones was bitterly disappointed when he learned that the Continental Congress had placed him eighteenth on the seniority list. One of Jones's failings as a naval officer, and as a human being, was his inability to distance himself from decisions that involved him or his career. Instead of appreciating that Congress was forced to appoint many men because they were well known in a particular geographic area and could thus generate support for the navy, Jones interpreted his ranking as a slight to his honor and abilities. Furious, he lashed out against those above him. In a letter to Robert Morris, a Pennsylvania delegate to Congress and a member of the Marine Committee, Jones charged that several of the officers promoted over him were "alto-gether illiterate and Utterly ignorant of Marine Affairs." In another letter, Jones argued that the new rankings slighted "the Gentleman or Man of Merit," by which Jones meant himself.

Moving on from the purely personal to important ideas on the naval service in general, Jones advocated that the Marine Committee consider a candidate's character and communication skills as much as technical expertise in promoting an officer to command a ship or a fleet. On another occasion, he proposed a system of promotion based on merit rather than political influence or nepotism, a farsighted reform that would be long in coming. Jones also advocated training schools for officers in the fleet and naval academies onshore. Although intemperate in some of what he wrote, Jones was enough of a patriot to say in his letters that he could not "think of quiting the Service" while "the liberties of America are Unconfirmed."

In 1777, Jones proposed a naval strategy that demonstrated his imagination, initiative, and audacity. Recognizing that the American navy was not strong enough to protect the country's coasts and that attacking British commercial shipping brought little strategic advantage, Jones and his patron, Robert Morris, championed a different role for the small, young American navy. As Morris stated in a letter to Jones, they believed that the navy's mission should be to "attack the Enemies defenceless places & thereby oblige them to Station more of their Ships in their own Countries." In other words, the navy should hit the British where they least expected it and where they were most vulnerable. Jones suggested leading a flotilla to Africa to harass the British African trade. Speaking for Congress, Robert Morris endorsed the main outline of Jones's plan but ordered an attack against British posts in the Caribbean, West Florida, and near the mouth of the Mississippi River.

The expedition never took place, however, and Jones blamed his old boss, naval commander Esek Hopkins. Jones was instead given command of the *Ranger*, a new sloop-of-war under construction at Portsmouth, New Hampshire. Jones and the *Ranger* were ordered to sail for Europe, which gave Jones the perfect opportunity to execute his plan to attack the British where they least expected it.

Thanks to Jones's efforts, the *Ranger* had the distinction of being the first vessel flying the Stars and Stripes to receive formal recognition from a foreign navy. On February 13, 1778, Jones anchored at France's Quiberon Bay, where a squadron of line-of-battle ships and three frigates under the command of French admiral La Motte Piquet were sitting at anchor awaiting to escort an American-bound convoy away from the European coast. Jones sent a note to La Motte Piquet saying he was prepared to discharge a thirteen-gun salute if the French would "Return Gun for Gun." It was an important moment, because the salute was "an Acknowlidgement of American Independence."

At about the same time, Jones received orders from Benjamin Franklin, Silas Deane, and Arthur Lee, the American commissioners in France. The orders the commissioners gave him, though vague, directed Jones to assault the enemy "by Sea, or otherwise." An earlier letter from Jones to the commissioners had spelled out his intentions:

> I have always since we have had Ships of War been persuaded that small Squadrons could be employed to far better Advantage on private expeditions and would distress the Enemy infinitely more than the same force could do by cruising either

Jointly or Seperately - were strict Secrecy Observed on our part the Enemy have many important Places in such a defenceless Situation that they might be effectually Surprised and Attacked with no considerable Force - We cannot yet Fight their Navy as their numbers and Force is so far Superiour to ours - therefore it seems to be our most natural Province to Surprize their defenceless places and thereby divide their attention and draw it off from our Coasts.

In a February 1778 letter to the commissioners, Jones reiterated his ideas, adding:

I have in contemplation several enterprizes of some importance - the Commissioners do not even promise to Justify me should I fail in any bold attempt - I will not however, under this discouragement, alter my designs. - When an Enemy think a design against them improbable they can always be Surprised and Attacked with Advantage. - it is true I must run great risque - but no Gallant action was ever performed without danger - therefore, tho' I cannot insure Success I will endeavour to deserve it.

As seen in these two letters, Jones understood that the Americans would have to fight the same kind of guerrilla war at sea as they were fighting on land. They could not engage the enemy fleet against fleet, nor was commerce raiding the answer. Although the latter might be profitable for the captains and crews, it would not significantly help the nation's interest. Striking the enemy where least expected would keep the British off balance and dispersed, forcing them to redeploy ships away from the American coast.

Jones's ideas were novel and reflected a patriotism that was willing to sacrifice personal gain and advancement for a greater good. His strategy did not appeal to his crew, however, who saw commercial raiding as their best chance to supplement their meager wages. On the *Ranger* and in his subsequent commands, Jones had problems with fractious crews because of his reputation as a risk taker and hard fighter who rejected raiding in favor of more perilous missions. In an effort to both mollify his crewmen and hurt the British by any means possible,

Jones agreed that they should capture merchant ships wherever possible so long as this did not detract from the overall strategic goal.

The cruise of the *Ranger*, which began in April 1778, was truly remarkable. It lasted twenty-eight days, and in that time, according to historian Samuel Eliot Morison, Jones, his crew, and his eighteen-gun ship "performed one of the most brilliant exploits of the naval war." In addition to taking two merchantmen and destroying several others, the *Ranger* captured a British man-of-war, took some two hundred prisoners, and most notably, executed a land raid that caught the public's attention in both England and America.

Jones had planned to raid a British coastal town as retaliation for English raids against towns on the Connecticut coast and in order to seize one or more important prisoners who might be exchanged for American seamen held in British prisons. The British government was willing to exchange captured American army officers and soldiers but insisted on treating naval prisoners as pirates with no rights. As a result, captured American seamen languished in British jails. The British could follow such a policy because American ships, especially privateers, captured few British prisoners and kept even fewer. Concerned with the fate of the captive American seamen, Jones hoped that by taking an English nobleman captive, he would force the British to authorize an exchange.

Jones mistakenly supposed that Lord Selkirk, his intended target, was a great lord whose detention would force the British to change their policy. Selkirk was, in fact, an unimportant Scottish peer. Moreover, he was away from home when Jones's raiding party arrived. Because of this, Jones—at the insistence of his crew—did nothing more than authorize his men to loot the Selkirk household silver. Jones refused to accompany his men on their mission and later purchased the silver from his men and returned it to the Selkirks, along with a lengthy apologetic letter spelling out the rationale for the raid.

The Selkirk raid roused the countryside and caused the Admiralty to send warships in pursuit of the *Ranger*. Jones, unaware that he was being chased, decided to attack the twenty-gun British ship *Drake*. It was basically an even match. The *Ranger* had more and heavier armament, but the *Drake* had more men. Jones decided to disable the *Drake* with cannon fire while preventing the British warship from closing with the *Ranger* and boarding it. In a battle lasting just over an hour, the *Ranger* forced the *Drake* to surrender. Jones, understanding the publicity value of bringing a British warship into a French port after his daring land raid, decided to take the *Drake* with him to France. For almost twenty-four hours, he remained off Whitehaven, England, refitting the damaged *Drake* before sailing for France via the northern tip of Ireland.

Reaction to the raid in England was interesting. Some publications characterized Jones as a bloodthirsty pirate interested only in murder and mayhem. These newspaper accounts even changed his physical appearance, describing Jones—who actually was about five foot, six inches, with light brown hair, fair skin, and hazel eyes—as being big, dark, and swarthy, like some fictional buccaneer from the Caribbean. Despite the attempts to demonize Jones, many saw him as a Robin Hood figure, who took from the upper classes but was considerate of working men. This impression was solidified when, on his return voyage to France, Jones set ashore fishermen he had earlier captured to gain knowledge of the local waters and reportedly gave them new sails and payment for their assistance.

With his success on the *Ranger*, Jones was given command of a squadron before returning to British waters. In September 1779, Jones served as captain of the *Bonhomme Richard*, an old converted merchant vessel, and commanded a "fleet" of three smaller warships in the waters off Scotland and northern England when he encountered a British convoy carrying naval stores to England from the Baltic Sea. Escorting the convoy were two British warships, the largest of which was the *Serapis*, fitted with fifty cannons and a crew of 284 men. A ship of that size and firepower occupied a place in the eighteenth-century Royal Navy equivalent to a cruiser in its twentieth-century counterpart. Jones decided to engage the *Serapis* in open battle a few miles off the point on the northeast English coastline known as Flamborough Head.

Clearly the *Bonhomme Richard* was at a serious disadvantage fighting a ship with such massively superior firepower and maneuverability. Moreover, an accident on the *Bonhomme Richard* greatly increased the odds of a British victory. While Jones's crew was firing the ship's second broadside, two of its biggest guns exploded. In his memoirs, Jones wrote that many of the officers and men working those guns, "who had been selected as the best of the crew," were killed, wounded, "or so frightened that none of them was of any use during the remainder of the engagement."

This accident left the *Bonhomme Richard* vulnerable to being blasted to pieces by the *Serapis*. Knowing it would be suicidal to continue to trade broadsides, Jones moved the *Bonhomme Richard* close to the enemy ship, allowing his crew to use grapples and lines to tie the ships together. But even with the two enemies locked in a death grip, the British gunners continued to fire into the *Bonhomme Richard* until her hull and lower decks were so battered that she looked more like a raft than a warship. In fact, the British gunners wreaked such devastation that they had to reposition their guns continually or their cannonballs would have passed completely through the *Bonhomme Richard* without hitting anything.

As the sea poured in through the holes in the hull, Jones's ship filled with water. With the long battle nearing its climax, the *Bonhomme Richard* lay half submerged. To keep her afloat, the master at arms released a hundred British prisoners, telling them to man the pumps and pump for their lives, or the vessel would sink and they would drown. But even their efforts could not keep pace with the incoming sea. The *Bonhomme Richard* was sinking.

As if the situation were not dire enough, fires raged both aloft in the sails and rigging and below deck. In fact, at times the fighting ceased so the crews of both vessels could combat the out-of-control blazes. Finally, the continual pounding inflicted by the *Serapis* had left half of Jones's crew dead or wounded. At this point in the battle, the senior warrant officer and ship's carpenter of the *Bonhomme Richard*, unable to see their captain or first lieutenant and assuming both were dead, decided to surrender their dying ship. They called for a cease-fire and ran to haul down the ship's pendant at the head of the mainmast. Hearing their calls for surrender, an enraged Jones drew his pistols and ran at them, shouting, "Shoot them, kill them!" The would-be surrenderers abandoned the ship's pendant and fled. Jones, finding his pistols unloaded, hurled his empty guns at the carpenter, striking him on the head and knocking him unconscious. The captain of the British warship, who had heard the calls for surrender, yelled across to Jones, "Have you struck? Do you call for Quarter?" Jones then replied, "I have not yet begun to fight," words that have defined the American navy ever since. With that, the battle continued, and although the odds against victory remained formidable, Jones's will to fight to the end reinvigorated his crew. They renewed the battle "with double fury" and succeeded in repelling a British boarding party.

The turning point of the battle occurred when a Scottish seaman serving on the *Bonhomme Richard* climbed down from the mainmast, moved along a spar to a point above the *Serapis*'s decks, and began to throw grenades onto the deck of the enemy ship. One of these grenades rolled down through a partially opened hatch and landed near cartridges that had been stacked along the portside gun. Because of the positions of the two ships, these guns were not in action, and the spare cartridges were piled behind them. The grenade's explosion ignited the cartridges, which in turn ignited other cartridges on the gun deck, creating a flash fire that had a devastating effect in the cramped gun deck filled with men and officers. Twenty crewmen died instantly, and another thirty were badly injured. Some of the men— their clothes burned off, their skin seared, and their hair on fire— jumped out of the ship's gun ports into the sea. With this explosion, the *Serapis*'s big guns fell silent.

When news of the disaster reached the *Serapis*'s captain, Richard Pearson, he decided to surrender and save his remaining crew from slaughter. Calling for quarter, he made his way to the rear of the warship and hauled down the battle ensign. Thus ended the three-and-a-half-hour battle. Jones and his men had prevailed and captured the *Serapis*. The badly damaged *Bonhomme Richard* sank shortly thereafter, but against long odds and a formidable foe, she and her crew had achieved a remarkable victory.

After the battle of Flamborough Head, Jones continued to elude British patrol ships and sailed into Texel, Holland, on October 3. Flamborough Head was the pinnacle of Jones's career, and his victory over the *Serapis* brought him the glory he had craved. But he reveled in it to the point of neglecting his command and his crew.

Shortly after arriving in Texel, Jones traveled to Amsterdam, where he was received as a hero. According to one of his midshipmen, Nathaniel Fanning, Jones "was treated as a conqueror. This so elated him with pride, that he had the vanity to go into the state house, mount the balcony or piazza, and shew himself in the front thereof, to the populace and people of distinction then walking on the public parade." Jones even worked as his own publicist to help further his fame. During October and November, he wrote dozens of letters, gave interviews, and helped get accounts of the battle published widely in European newspapers. As a side benefit, this publicity helped further the American cause. The problem was that Jones focused on it to the detriment of his command. As a friend and American agent in the Netherlands warned him in an October 18 letter:

> I have seen persons of authority here who are warm friends of America and who have spoken to me much about your squadron. Their opinion is that you did not do wrong to come and show yourself here; but, on the other had, they think that you should not repeat this step, because that would give you too much publicity and it would produce a bad effect. . . . I must warn you also, my dear sir, that these same friends told me something which, whether or not it is true, hurts me as much as it does them, namely that, according to what one says, there reigns a great filth and infection in the Serapis; people have seen pieces of cadavers left from the battle. . . . This shocks people here right now and makes one fear the consequences of such negligence. In the name of God, my dear sir, put order in all this. Do not leave your ship again. Have it cleaned and purged of this filth.

Jones's quest for fame led him to diminish unfairly the contributions made by fellow officers during the engagement with the *Serapis*. One of the captains in Jones's squadron, Denis-Nicholas Cottineau, whom Jones considered a friend, wrote a memoir that was highly critical of Jones's insufferable self-promotion. As Cottineau wrote on November 15, 1779, "Ungrateful to his crew, he makes it seem that he alone did everything." Nor was this a new development. Throughout his service in the Continental Navy, Jones was slow to credit subordinates or superiors and quick to criticize them. As a result, he comes across as having been ungrateful, supersensitive, and self-absorbed.

A more serious incident also originated in Jones's self-absorption. In June 1780, Jones took command of the frigate *Alliance* and slipped out of Texel, eluding a blockading English squadron. He went to Spain and then to Lorient, France, to refit. While the *Alliance* was at Lorient,

Jones traveled to Paris, where he promoted himself so effectively that King Louis XVI awarded him the Order of Military Merit and gave him a gold sword. In Jones's absence, Pierre Landais, the former commander of the *Alliance*, whom Jones had charged with treachery at the battle of Flamborough Head, boarded the ship and convinced the crew that Jones was trying to rob them of prize money and that he, Landais, was their only hope for returning to America. With Landais in command, the *Alliance* sailed for America, leaving Jones behind.

Jones blamed port officials at Lorient for not stopping Landais, but a letter from Benjamin Franklin, America's minister to France and Jones's patron and friend, reveals the damning truth:

> If you had stayed on board where your duty lay, instead of coming to Paris, you would not have lost your ship. Now you blame them [the port officers] as having deserted you in recovering her; though relinquishing to prevent mischief was a voluntary act of your own, for which you have credit; hereafter, if you should observe an occasion to give your officers and friends a little more praise than is their due, and confess more fault than you can justly be charged with, you will only become the sooner for it, a great captain. Criticizing and censuring almost every one you have to do with, will diminish friends, increase enemies, and thereby hurt your affairs.

Having lost another ship and another command, Jones now was given command of the *Ariel*, a corvette built for the British navy but seized by the French and loaned to the Americans as a supply ship. On taking command, Jones decided the vessel needed to be rerigged to improve its sailing abilities. The changes delayed his departure to America, and by the time the *Ariel* finally set sail in September 1780, the weather had changed. She was caught in a vicious gale that battered the French coast and destroyed numerous ships. The *Ariel* survived thanks to Jones's superior seamanship, but she lost two masts and had to return to Lorient for repair, keeping Jones and the vessel in France until February 1781.

Jones honestly believed he would be received as a hero in America and must have been stunned beyond words when he was met with a congressional investigation. Certain delegates, hoping to use Jones's

conduct in France as a means to discredit Franklin, initiated an investigation into whether Jones had unnecessarily delayed the shipment of
war supplies to America. Quickly deciding that the investigation would
not achieve what they hoped, the delegates abandoned the inquiry and
turned the matter over to the Board of Admiralty. The secretary of the
board submitted forty-seven questions to Jones, who, as a master of
self-promotion, skillfully answered them, highlighting his triumphs
and blaming any problems on others, most notably Pierre Landais.

Jones's triumph was confirmed when the French ambassador conferred on him the *Order du Mérite Militaire*, the highest award the
French could give to a foreigner. Congress then voted a resolution of
thanks to Jones and gave him command of the *America*, the Continental Navy's only ship-of-the-line, which was then being built at
Portsmouth, New Hampshire.

Jones hoped to use the *America* as the flagship of a flotilla that
would again attack England, but on arriving at Portsmouth, he was
shocked to find progress on the vessel "backward." While Jones
actively supervised construction and the procurement of craftsmen
and materials needed to complete the vessel, inadequate funds from
the near-bankrupt continental government meant that work on
the *America* progressed sporadically and slowly. In the end, a cash-
strapped Congress presented the *America* to the French as a replacement for a French man-of-war that had been destroyed on a sandbar
outside of Boston Harbor.

The failure to complete the *America* in time for active duty, and the
intrigue of Jones's naval enemies, denied him his fondest dream—a
rear admiral's rank in the Continental Navy. He spent the remaining
years of his life trying to increase his professional knowledge of fleet
command and convince Congress that he should be appointed the
U.S. Navy's first admiral. He sought and received permission to travel
to Europe, ostensibly to recover prize money owed to the officers and
men of the *Bonhomme Richard* and serve as a reminder of the American
navy in European capitals. He again sought an admiral's commission
to enhance his prestige, but the title would have been an honorary
one at best, because the United States had no navy at the time. Captains who were senior to him blocked the request.

Frustrated, Jones left America in 1788 and sailed to Denmark to
obtain additional prize money. While in Denmark, he was offered a

commission in the Imperial Russian Navy. Attracted by the opportunity to command a fleet and hoping that his new title would impress Congress enough to award him an admiral's rank, Jones accepted the offer and set out for St. Petersburg.

The Russians sent Jones to the Black Sea, where the new rear admiral believed he would command all the naval forces in that theater in their operations against the Turks, but he discovered that three other rear admirals served in the command and each jealously guarded his power and privileges. Jones was instrumental in the Russian naval victory at Liman, but another admiral, Prince Nassau-Siegen, a friend of Empress Catherine II's key advisor, Prince Potemkin, usurped all credit for the victory. Jones was recalled to Moscow, where a probably trumped-up sex charge linking Jones and a young girl scandalized the empress and ended any chances for his restoration to command.

In the end, Jones returned to Paris, where he remained without money or prospects and was all but ignored until his death in July 1792 at age forty-five from an unknown illness. John Paul Jones was buried in Paris, and the site of his grave was forgotten until 1905, when his remains were returned to the United States to be reinterred in a magnificent tomb at the United States Naval Academy in Annapolis, Maryland. Here his presence remains a symbol for the U.S. Navy and those who have served in it.

Afterword

Even as this book goes to press in 2012, the legal system in Virginia is once again having to contend with acts of piracy. Eleven men from Somalia fired on a U.S. Navy vessel in a late-night attack, mistakenly thinking it was a merchant ship. The navy vessel responded instantly and captured the accused pirates, who were taken to Virginia for trial. If convicted of piracy or attempted piracy, they will receive life sentences. Apparently, the penalty for a piracy conviction is no longer automatically a public hanging. This is the first trial for piracy that has taken place in Virginia since the American Civil War. Meanwhile, a group of ten alleged Somali pirates, who attacked a German cargo ship and were taken captive by Dutch navy commandos, face trial in Germany for their accused crimes. So long as valuable cargo crosses the ocean, it will be tempting prey to individuals who feel they have nothing left to lose. And so long as pirates hunt merchant shipping vessels, pirate hunters will be in hot pursuit.

Glossary

Barquentine   Barque

Barkentine (barquentine) and bark (barque). The barkentine and bark were both medium-size, three-masted ships generally ranging between 120 and 160 feet in length. The barkentine was distinguished from the bark in that the front (fore) mast of the barkentine was square rigged, and the two rear masts were fore-and-aft rigged. When the same type of ship had the fore mast and middle (main) mast rigged with square sails and only the rear mast fore-and-aft rigged, it was referred to as a bark. Larger and heavier than either the sloop or schooner, the barkentine was capable of carrying more and heavier cannons, but its size made it slower than these other ships. The barkentine's size and weight also made it unsuitable for shallow inlets and river navigation. Designed as a merchant vessel, this ship could be converted for military or privateer use when rigged with fore-and-aft sails.

Brigantine   Brig

Brigantine and brig. The brigantine and brig were identical in structure: two-masted ships ranging between 110 and 140 feet in length and requiring a crew of 100 to 150 men to operate. The difference in designation between the two was the sail arrangement. When set with square rigging on the front (fore) mast and fore-and-aft rigging on the rear mast, the ship was referred to as a brigantine; when set with square rigging on both masts and a single fore-and-aft sail running behind the rear mast, it became a brig. Both versions were popular as trading vessels, and both were used for military purposes, with the brig rigging being the more popular arrangement for military use. A fully armed brig or brigantine could carry up to twenty 32-pounder cannons. Smaller, faster, and lighter than either the man-of-war or ship-of-the-line, the brig was an ideal pursuit vessel for chasing pirates and privateers.

Cannon. Whereas modern cannons are measured in caliber, seventeenth- and eighteenth-century cannons were measured according to the weight of the balls they fired. For instance, a six-pounder cannon fired balls weighing six pounds. Eighteenth-century naval cannons generally came in eight sizes: six-, nine-, twelve-, eighteen-, twenty-four-, thirty-two-, forty-two-, and two hundred-pounders. The balls ranged in diameter from 3.67 inches for the six-pounder to 8 inches for the two hundred-pounder.

Cannon, naval. Although the barrels of naval cannons were similar in size and weight to field cannons, the carriages on which they were mounted were much lower than those of cannons used in field battles. The wheels on which the beds rested were normally no more than eight to twelve inches in diameter.

Frigate

Corvette. A corvette was a two-masted sloop converted for military or privateer use and rigged with a combination of square and fore-and-aft sails. Corvettes tended to be between forty and sixty feet in length. They were lightly armed with any number of swivel guns and six to eighteen lightweight cannons, all of which were mounted on the main deck. Fast, light, and easy to maneuver, the corvette was ideal for privateers and coastal patrols.

Cutter. Similar to the sloop in appearance, the cutter was a single-masted vessel that differed from the sloop only in that its single mast was located farther back on the ship. For further information, see *sloop*.

Frigate. A medium-size, three-masted, square-rigged warship, the frigate was smaller than the man-of-war and carried fewer cannons. Frigates tended to be 180 to 220 feet long and 46 to 50 feet wide, with an average below-the-waterline depth of 20 feet. The frigate's complement of twenty-eight to sixty cannons was located on its single gun deck, located directly below the upper deck. Under the direction of a skilled captain, a frigate could maneuver almost as well as a schooner and run faster than the sleekest merchant ship of the day. Frigates were first brought into service in 1757 by Britain's Royal Navy, which had sixty frigates by the time of the American Revolution.

Grapeshot. Grapeshot refers to small, round iron balls that could be fired from cannons as antipersonnel shot. They were similar in size to musket balls, about three-quarters of an inch in diameter. Grapeshot was usually banded together for ease of loading into the gun. When the gun was fired, the band would snap, allowing the shot to spread out for maximum dispersion.

Man of War

Letter of marque. A letter of marque was an official document issued by a government to a private citizen, giving the recipient and those in his employ the right to seize or destroy the goods or property of an enemy nation or of individuals employed by an enemy nation.

Longboat. Also known as a jolly boat or barge, the longboat was the primary means of moving men and equipment between a large ship and the shore or between two large ships. Longboats ranged from twenty to twenty-eight feet long and averaged between seven and nine feet wide. Although some longboats were fitted with detachable masts and could be rigged for sail, their primary means of propulsion was by oar. Longboat oarsmen rowed in pairs, with two individuals manning each of the boat's six to eight pairs of oars. A longboat crew generally consisted of the required number of oarsmen plus one officer manning the tiller (located in the rear of the boat), which steered the craft. When necessary, a longboat could also accommodate as many passengers as oarsmen, bringing the largest longboat's capacity to thirty-three men.

Man-of-war or man-o'-war. A heavily armed, three-masted warship with square-rigged sails, the man-of-war (also spelled man-o'-war) was the primary battleship from the mid-seventeenth to early nineteenth century. A full-size man-of-war could be up to two hundred feet in length and carry anywhere from seventy-four to a hundred cannons mounted on three tiers of gun decks.

Periagua. In the Caribbean and on the Eastern Seaboard of North America, periagua (from the Spanish word *piragua*, in turn derived from the Carib language term for dugout), formerly referred to a range of small craft, including canoes and sailing vessels. By the eighteenth century, the term was applied to flat-bottomed boats that had one or two masts and could also be rowed. These boats could be thirty feet or more long and carried up to thirty men. Benjamin Hornigold and Sam Bellamy began their careers as pirate captains operating from periaguas.

Pink. In the Atlantic Ocean, pink (derived from the Dutch word *pincke*) referred to any small ship with a narrow stern. Pinks had a large cargo capacity and were generally square rigged. Their flat bottoms and resulting shallow draft made them more useful in shallow waters than some similar classes of ship. They were most often used for short-range missions in protected channels, as both merchant vessels and warships. A number saw service in the Royal Navy during the second half of the seventeenth century. This style of ship was often used in the Mediterranean because it could navigate in shallow waters and through coral reefs. It could also be maneuvered up rivers and streams. Contrary to popular thought, the pink is quite a fast and flexible ship.

Pinnace. The term *pinnace* could refer to two different types of marine craft. The first was a small vessel used as a "tender" to larger vessels, among other things, and the second was a ship-rigged vessel popular in northern waters in the seventeenth through nineteenth centuries. The smaller pinnace was a lightweight boat, propelled by sails or oars, formerly used as a tender for guiding merchant and war vessels. In modern parlance, *pinnace* has come to mean a boat associated with some kind of larger vessel that doesn't fit under the launch or lifeboat definitions. In general, the pinnace had sails and was employed to ferry messages between ships-of-the-line, visit harbors ahead of the fleet with messages of state, pick up mail, and so on. Pinnaces were also widely used during the pirate-infested seventeenth century, mostly in the Caribbean area. The Spanish favored them as lightweight smuggling vessels, whereas the Dutch preferred them as raiders. Pirates frequently employed them as scouts and for night attacks, since they were small, reliable, and extremely quick, even against the wind. The second, larger type was developed by the Dutch during the early seventeenth century. It had a hull form resembling a small "race-built" galleon and was usually rigged as a ship (square rigged on three masts) or carried a similar rig on two masts, in a fashion akin to the later brig. Pinnaces saw use as merchant vessels, pirate vessels, and small warships. Not all were small vessels, some being nearer to larger ships in tonnage. This type saw widespread use in northern waters, mainly by the Dutch.

Rigging. Rigging as a general term describes both the ropes and block-and-tackle used to control and support the sails of a ship. Sailing ships of the seventeenth and eighteenth centuries carried their sails in one of two manners: either square rigged or fore-and-aft rigged. In the fore-and-aft rig, the sails were arranged to stand along the length of the ship, from bow to stern, whereas in the square-rig arrangement, the sails ran perpendicularly across the ship from port to starboard (left to right). Large warships and merchant ships with three masts were almost universally square rigged, because this type of arrangement tended to work better on the long sea voyages for which they were designed. Small ships, such as sloops and schooners, were normally fore-and-aft rigged for greater maneuverability. On some vessels, such as cutters, a combination of square and fore-and-aft rigging was used. In other cases, the type of rigging determined the ship's designation; for example, when square rigged, some two-masted ships were known as brigantines, but when the same ships carried a combination of square and fore-and-aft rigging, they were called brigs.

Schooner. Schooners were medium-size, two-masted ships that were usually fore-and-aft rigged. Almost as fast and maneuverable as sloops, schooners were a particular favorite in the American coastal mercantile trade, and they adapted well for privateering use. Easily manned by small crews, schooners tended to be between 120 and 160 feet long and from 32 to 36 feet wide. They were shallow drafted, with a depth below the waterline of 10 to 14

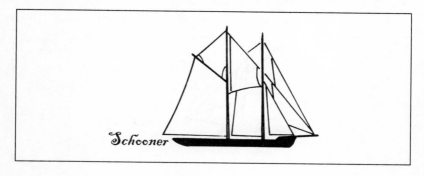

Schooner

feet, making them easy to navigate in shallow rivers and inlets, where larger ships could not follow. An armed privateer schooner could carry six to ten small-bore cannons on its main deck.

Ship-of-the-line. The largest of the men-of-war, Britain's ships-of-the-line were the largest, most dangerous vessels afloat. A ship-of-the-line could carry 74 to 124 cannons on three gun decks, although the most common (about fifty percent of the Royal Navy) carried only 74 guns, with 35 located on each side of the ship on the gun decks and 2 on the top deck. The size and weight of a ship-of-the-line allowed it to carry a preponderance of heavy cannons, ranging in size from thirty-two- to forty-two-pounders. A typical ship-of-the-line during the mid-eighteenth century had a crew of more than eight hundred men. Ships-of-the-line got their name from the battle tactic wherein the vessels in a fleet would form in a long line, rather than be confined in a cluster, so that they could sail past an enemy one after the other, raking an enemy ship with an unbroken line of fire.

Sloop. A sloop was a small, easily maneuvered, fore-and-aft rigged ship with a single mast requiring only a small crew to man. The sloop was distinguished from a cutter by the position of its mast, which was located only about one-third of the ship's length behind the bow, placing it farther forward than the cutter's mast. The sloop generally carried three sails: a large main sail, extending to the back of the mast, and two triangular sails running from the mast to the front of the ship. Sloops could range in length from thirty to sixty feet. Although a sloop could carry only six to ten small cannons, its speed and maneuverability allowed it to attack and outrun larger ships with heavier armament.

Swivel gun. Small, portable cannons mounted on Y-shaped forks, swivel guns were usually less than three feet long and normally had bores of one and a quarter inches. A swivel gun could fire either a single ball or a handful of grapeshot. The butt end of the gun was usually fitted with a wooden handle so that the gunner could easily turn and aim the gun after dropping the bottom leg of the fork into a hole in a ship's railing or an oarlock on a whaleboat or longboat. Relatively lightweight, the swivel gun could be carried by one man from one side of a ship to the other or onto a whaleboat or longboat.

Tonnage. A ship's tonnage refers to its size. It does not describe the weight of the ship, but is a measurement of the amount of water the ship displaces based on the fact that a hundred cubic feet of seawater weighs one Imperial British long-ton (tonne), or 2,240 pounds. Because a ship rides lower in the water when fully loaded than it does when empty—and therefore displaces more water—the tonnage is calculated when the craft is fully loaded.

Whaleboat. The fast and highly maneuverable whaleboat's speed was aided by its shallow draft and the fact that it was pointed at both ends like a canoe. An additional advantage of the double prow (points on both ends) was the fact that the whaleboat did not have to be turned around to reverse direction—the oarsmen could simply turn around in their seats and continue rowing. Whaleboats were all propelled by oars rather than sails. Originally designed to be carried on whaling ships and lowered into the water when a whale was sighted, the whaleboat adapted wonderfully to coastal privateering. Enhancing the whaleboat's ability to hide from pursuers was its retractable keel, which allowed it to navigate shallow rivers, shoals, and sandbar-filled coastal waters where larger, deeper vessels could not follow. Averaging thirty-six feet in length, the whaleboats could be manned by as few as six men but, as needs dictated, could carry as many as twenty-four.

Bibliography

Bonner, Willard Haliam. *Pirate Laureate: The Life and Legends of Captain Kidd.* New Brunswick, NJ: Rutgers University Press, 1947.

Breverton, Terry. *Black Bart Roberts: The Greatest Pirate of Them All.* Bro Morgannwg, Wales, UK: Glyndwr Publishing, 2004.

Burgess, Paul C. *The Annals of Brigantine.* Atlantic City, NJ: Joseph Josephson, 1964.

Burl, Aubrey. *Black Barty: Bartholomew Roberts and His Pirate Crew 1718–1723.* Stroud, England: Sutton Publishing, 2006.

Burney, James (Capt.). *History of the Buccaneers of America.* London: Payne and Foss, 1816.

Cawthorne, Nigel. *Pirates: An Illustrated History.* Great Malvern, England: Capella Publishing, 2005.

Coggleshall, George. *History of the American Privateers and Letters of Marque During our War with England in the Years 1812, '13, and '14.* New York: Putnam, 1861.

Cordingly, David. *Life Among the Pirates: The Romance and the Reality.* New York: Little Brown and Company, 1995.

———. *Under The Black Flag: The Romance and Reality of Life Among the Pirates.* London: Harcourt Brace & Co., 1995.

Crooker, William S. *Pirates of the North Atlantic.* Halifax, NS, Canada: Nimbus Publishing, 2004.

Dampier, William. *Piracy, Turtles & Flying Foxes.* 1686. Reprint, London: Penguin Books, 2007.

Diehl, Daniel, and Mark Donnelly. *How Did They Manage? Leadership Secrets of History.* London: Spiro Press, 2002.

Donnelly, Mark, and Daniel Diehl. *Pirates of New Jersey: Plunder and High Adventure on the Garden State Coastline.* Mechanicsburg, PA: Stackpole Books, 2010.

Earle, Peter. *The Pirate Wars.* New York: Methuen Books, 2004.

Ellms, Charles. *Pirates: Authentic Narratives of the Lives, Exploits, and Executions of the World's Most Infamous Buccaneers.* New York: Random House Value, 1996.

Exquemelin, Alexander. *The Buccaneers of America*. New York: Dover Publications, 1969.

Gilbert, Henry. *Pirates: True Tales of Notorious Buccaneers*. New York: Dover Publications, 2008.

Grosse, Philip. *The Pirates' Who's Who: Giving Particulars Of The Lives and Deaths Of The Pirates And Buccaneers*. New York: Burt Franklin, 1924.

Herrmann, Oscar. *Pirates and Piracy*. New York: Stettiner Brothers, 1902.

Johnson, Captain Charles. *A General History of the Robberies & Murders of the Most Notorious Pirates*. 1724. Reprint, London: Conway Maritime Press, 1998.

Lewis, Jon E., ed. *The Mammoth Book of Pirates*. London: Constable Robinson, 2006.

Little, Benerson. *The Sea Rover's Practice: Pirate Tactics and Techniques, 1630–1730*. Washington, DC: Potomac Books, 2005.

Lucie-Smith, Edward. *Outcasts of the Sea: Pirates and Piracy*. New York: Paddington Press, 1978.

Maclay, Edward Stanton. *A History of American Privateers*. New York: D. Appleton and Company, 1899.

Masefield, John. *On the Spanish Main: Or, some English Forays on the Isthmus of Darien*. London: Methuen and Co., 1906.

Mitchell, David. *Pirates*. London: Book Club Associates, 1976.

Nash, Jay Robert. *The Encyclopedia of World Crime*. New York: Crime Books, 1990.

Norman, C. B. *The Corsairs of France*. London: Searle & Rivington, 1887.

Patton, Robert H. *Patriot Pirates: The Privateer War for Freedom and Fortune in the American Revolution*. New York: Pantheon Books, 2008.

Pirotta, Saviour. *Pirates and Treasures*. Andover, Hampshire, UK: Thomson Learning, 1995.

Platt, Richard. *Pirate*. New York: Alfred A. Knopf, 1994.

Pyle, Howard. *Howard Pyle's Book of Pirates*. New York: Dover Books, 2000.

Pyle, Howard, ed. *The Buccaneers and Marooners of America*. London: T. Fisher Unwin, 1892.

Rediker, Marcus. *Villains of All Nations: Atlantic Pirates in the Golden Age*. Boston: Beacon Press, 2004.

Richards, Stanley. *Black Bart*. Swansea, Wales, UK: Christopher Davies, 1966.

Roberts, Nancy. *Blackbeard and Other Pirates of the Atlantic Coast*. Winston-Salem, NC: John F. Blair Publisher, 1995.

Rogers, Captain Woodes. *Life Aboard a British Privateer in the time of Queen Anne*. London: Chapman and Hall, 1889.

Rogozinski, Jan. *Honor Among Thieves: Captain Kidd, Henry Every, and the Pirate Democracy in the Indian Ocean*. Mechanicsburg, PA: Stackpole Books, 2000.

Sanders, Richard. *If a Pirate I Must Be . . . The True Story of "Black Bart," King of the Caribbean Pirates*. London: Aurum Press, 2007.

Seitz, Don C. *Under the Black Flag: Exploits of the Most Notorious Pirates.* New York: The Dial Press, 1925.

Shomette, Donald G. *Pirates on the Chesapeake: Being a True History of Pirates, Picaroons, and Raiders on Chesapeake Bay, 1610–1807.* Centreville, MD: Tidewater Publishers, 1985.

Stark, Francis R. *The Abolition of Privateering and the Declaration of Paris.* New York: Columbia University, 1897.

Stivers, Reuben Elmore. *Privateers and Volunteers.* Annapolis, MD: Naval Institute Press, 1975.

Stockton, Frank R. *Buccaneers and Pirates of our Coasts.* London: Macmillian and Co., 1919.

Thomas, Evan. *John Paul Jones: Sailor, Hero, Father of the American Navy.* New York: Simon and Schuster, 2003.

Thornbury, Walter. *The Monarchs of the Main.* London: Routledge, 1861.

Winston, Alexander. *Pirates and Privateers.* London: Arrow Books, 1969.

Woodard, Colin. *The Republic of Pirates.* New York: Harcourt Brace, 2007.

Zacks, Richard. *The Pirate Hunter: The True Story of Captain Kidd.* New York: Hyperion Books, 2002.

ONLINE SOURCES

http://www.piratedocuments.com
http://www.njhm.com/captainkiddstory.htm
http://www.bio.umass.edu/biology/conn.river/kidd.html
http://colonial-america.suite101.com/article.cfm/the_trial_of_captain_kidd
http://www.thepiratesrealm.com/Captain%20Kidd%20Stockton.html
http://www.associatedcontent.com/article/423917/rep_alan_bennys_clues_to_pirate_captain.html
http://www.blacksheepancestors.com/pirates/
http://www.mainlesson.com/display.php?author=stockton&book=buccaneers&story=kidd
http://bestoflegends.org/pirates/kidd.html
http://www.elizabethan-era.org.uk/blackbeard.htm
http://www.republicofpirates.net/Blackbeard.html
http://americanhistory.suite101.com/article.cfm/the_man_known_as_blackbeard_or_edward_teach#ixzz0bjwMJCc2
http://www.famouswelsh.com/Welsh-Adventure/Profiles/Pirate_Black_Bart_01.php
http://www.thewayofthepirates.com/famous-pirates/bartholomew-roberts.php
http://brethrencoast.com/bio/roberts.html
http://njpiratehi.tripod.com/brtrbrts.html
http://www.thepirateking.com/bios/index.htm